11.9.99.

The Complete Beginn... ...o The

World Wide Web

Scott Western

NET.WORKS

NET.WORKS

**Net.Works, PO Box 200
Harrogate, N.Yorks
HG1 2YR   England
Email: sales@net-works.co.uk
UK Fax: 01423-526035**

Net.Works is an imprint of Take That Ltd.

ISBN: 1 873668 51 1
Design © 1998 Take That Ltd.
Text ©1998 Scott Western

First Edition March 1998

Trademarks:
Trademarked names are used throughout this book. Rather than place a trademark symbol in every occurance of a trademark name, the names are being used only in an editorial fashion for the benefit of the trademark owner, with no intention to infringe the trademark.

Printed and bound in The United Kingdom

Disclaimer:
The information in this book is distributed on an "as is" basis, without warranty. While very effort has been made to ensure that this book is free from errors or omissions, neither the author, the publisher, or their respective employees and agents, shall have any liability to any person or entity with respect to any liability, loss or damage caused or alleged to have been caused directly or indirectly by advice or instructions contained in this book or by the computer hardware or software products described herein. **Readers are urged to seek prior expert advice before making decisions, or refraining from making decisions, based on information or advice contained in this book.**

Throughout this book you will find web addresses on various subjects. These will start you off on your journey around the WWW. However, just like 'real life' addresses, some may have changed since going to press. We hope this does not spoil your enjoyment.

Contents

Introduction

The World Wide Web

THE WORLD WIDE WEB (**WWW**, or **Web** for short) has virtually taken over the Internet, and for many people is The Internet. It is hard to believe that only a few years ago even the most informed experts were saying that the World Wide Web would not survive to the end of the Millennium. Little did they know the Internet would expand at such a rate that even the most computer illiterate would be sucked into its hype. Once this has happened, as with all other media, the need for pictures and easy-to-read contents rapidly overtook the more serious resources on the Internet.

With so many people surfing the Web it did not take long for Big Business to see it as a new way of selling around the globe. Simply by putting their wears onto a computer they could allow people to shop at their leisure and buy their products in the comfort of their own home. It also captured the imagination of educators as a way of getting quite detailed information across to a large audience.

Before joining the World Wide Web you may have wondered what all the fuss was about when you heard the word "**Browser**". But it was the introduction

http://www.bbc.co.uk

of these Browsers, used to navigate the World Wide Web, which "hid away" the cold, dry collection of commands that computers need to speak to one another. So instead of having to type long commands and selecting from plain text menus, now you can use your mouse to click away

Welcome to the Tesco Website.

Home Shopping extended to 5 more London Stores

Internet Superstore   Baby & Toddler

Gift Delivery Service   Financial Services

Drinks Collection   Free Software

Recipe Collection   TESCO   Information

Every little helps.

Groceries have hit the Web at
http://www.tesco.co.uk

in a GUI (Graphical User Interface) environment. You could say that it is the arrival of Browsers which brought the masses to the Internet.

Now you can sit at home with your computer plugged into a telephone socket and click your way across the globe.

By simply lifting one finger (and pressing it down again) you can receive information on virtually any subject you can think about. And to access this information you require virtually no technical understanding of how you are receiving it or where it is coming from. What is more, you can acces it when YOU want. There's no viewing schedules for the Web!

Life on the Web

Would you say you look for-ward to your weekly shopping - getting into the car after a hard day at work, driving through the rain and then doing battle with millions of other shoppers desperately trying to find the one product that you require hidden away in the darkest corner of the supermarket, and then standing for six years at the Express Check-out only to find you left your wallet or purse at home?

Well that is thing of the past. Now you can order your groceries on the World Wide Web and have them delivered directly to your door!

If you are after a particular book but fed up with going around bookshops and being confronted with massive piles of the latest hyped paperback, then your problems could be solved. Visit one of the many bookshops on the World Wide Web and type in the title, or even one word of the title and you will find details of the book within seconds. And, just as with your groceries, you will be able to order on-line and have them delivered to your door.

And it does not stop there. You can order virtually any type of goods that you like from CD's to fusion splicers, and from underwear to lottery machines. You can read newspapers (containing only the news items you are interested in) and even watch the broadcasts on-line.

You can gamble all your money away or tour around one of the hundreds of museums and galleries. You can try out the latest software and download it straight on to your computer. Then you can contact support staff or pick up the latest patch to make it work better.

On-line banking via the Web is with us already. If you want to find out your current balance, transfer money between accounts, pay a few bills or raise a loan you can do it all using your computer on a connection to the Web. No more queuing whilst somebody pays in £600 worth of 5p pieces they have been collecting for the last 32 years, or while a financial illiterate tries to come to terms with their latest statement. No more paperwork, and no more degrading looks from the clerks.

Feeling a bit under the weather? Then why not visit a doctor. Don't go looking for the car keys, just log onto the Web. More and more doctor's surgeries are creating an Internet presence and offer diagnosis and helpful information via the World Wide Web, and it won't be long before this virtual doctor will send you a prescription straight back to your printer. Better still, they may E-mail you the prescription which you then forward on to a pharmacy with a Web presence who then deliver the pills through your letter box!

Once you are cured you can go out and live it up. But first check out the restaurants in your area by consulting one of the many search engines on the Web. Take a look at their menus and book a table before you even pick up your car keys. Then nip over to a site which reviews films or plays to take in before your meal.

If your travels are further afield, then you can forget going down the high street to visit the travel agent. Browse the travel company's brochures at your leisure on-line and find that dream holiday you have always been looking for. And visit one or two airlines and decide on some flights that will suit you rather than the package company. Then finally book the tickets direct or visit one of the many travel agents who offer their facilities on the WWW.

Do you need a gardner? a plumber? or a builder to knock up a quick conservatory? then you know where to look.

Myth: The WWW is only for men without social lives.

Truth: The biggest Web user growth is coming from students and families.

Chapter 1

Getting on the Web

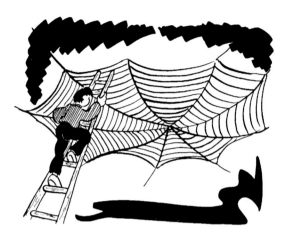

SURFING THE NET these days really is easy. In the early days setting up your computer system and, more to the point, loading the software necessary to join the Internet was a nightmare. The relevant browsers (software used to 'see' pages on the WWW) were created for a few systems, such as UNIX mainframes. So versions created for use on personal computers weren't well supported and fell over regularly.

The worst part was getting different software programs to 'talk' to one another on your computer and then communicate everything to your modem. This was hugely ironic, considering the Internet was created so all computers could 'talk' to one another in the same language wherever they are (see *Complete Beginner's Guide to the Internet*, details page 111).

The Internet being the beast that it is, everything has progressed at frightening speed. In just a couple of years, manufacturers have started talking to one another, benchmarks have been created and standard formats agreed. Well, almost.

So now, most software packages are compatible. Load a new browser and it will almost certainly work with your dialer software. Add an FTP program (used for transferring files) and it will slot in beside the browser and dialer.

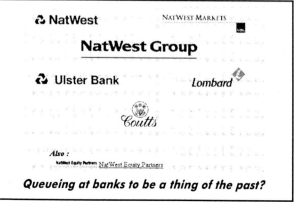

Queueing at banks to be a thing of the past?

Enough of the chat. This is what you need to start surfing:

Computer

The most obvious item required for access to the WWW is, of course, a **computer**. Make sure that it is 'up to speed'. Whilst "old faithful" may do an adequate job for you on day to day word processing, it may be totally useless when it comes to the WWW.

The WWW is all about cool imagery (static and moving), video clips and sounds used to entertain and transmit useful information- so speed is a crucial factor. Old faithful may output one or two letters a day but could it cope with downloading a large graphics file from a flashy new site?

In essence you are going to need a computer that has been built in the last two years. Probably with a 486 or a **Pentium** chip, at least **eight Meg of RAM** and a suitable **hard disk of over 500 Meg**. This last item is necessary to store the software you will be using to connect to your ISP and store any information or programs that you will download from the WWW. Remember you'll find tons of useful, and useless, software and images that you'll want to obtain from the Web - so you'll need somewhere to put it all!

A non-essential accessory is a **sound card**. Many sites now incorporate sounds into their pages, so you hear music or commentary as you move around. You'll need a sound board and speakers.

If you do not already have a computer or are looking to upgrade your existing computer expect to pay £500 - £1,000 for a reasonably speedy, up-to-date machine. Anything less may look a bargain but could prove a hindrance later on as modems improve, bandwidth expands and sites go for a full multimedia approach.

Modem

Notwithstanding the above, the single most important piece of equipment for your connection to the WWW is your **Modem**. A slow computer will still be quick enough to deal with information it receives swifter than your modem can accept it

A modem is a device that lets your computer "talk" down a telephone line to another computer. At the other end of the telephone line will be another modem which accepts your call and connects you to a computer which is **permanently** connected to 'The Internet'. Once 'joined' together, your computer becomes another part of the Net.

It can come in one of two forms. It can either be a card which is inserted into your computer . You then simply connect your telephone line

★ Market Size	Service Provider	Estimated Number of 'Live' UK Subscribers
UK and World User Demographics, Attitudes	CompuServe	350,000-400,000
	AOL	230,000-250,000
The UK ISP Subscriber League Table	Microsoft Network (UK)	130,000-140,000
	Demon	120,000-130,000
Advertising on the Internet	BT Internet	70,000-85,000
Electronic Commerce	UUNET Pipex Dial	45,000-50,000
Online Ad Rates	Global Internet	35,000-42,000
	Virgin Net	30,000-55,000
Ad Sales Networks	EasyNet Group	23,000-28,000
Site Measurement and Audit	LineOne	19,000-30,000
	Direct Connection	23,500-25,000
Marketing News and Information Sources	U-Net	15,000-20,000
	Netcom	18,000-25,000
Seven Laws of CyberAds	Cable Internet	14,000-18,000
Events	Prestel Online	10,000-13,000
	Enterprise	11,000-12,000
Charts of Hot Sites	I-Way	8,000-9,000
Search Tools	Which?Online	10,000-12,000
	Source: EMAP Online's Internet Marketing Hot List	

EMAPs ISP Subscriber leage table http://www.internet-sales/hot

into the back of your computer when you want to use it. Or it can be a stand alone modem which will either sit on your desk top or on the floor underneath your computer.

And that is basically all it does. It translates your computer's data into audio tones, called modulation, and then converts audio tones back into electronic data, called demodulation.

Since all modems essentially do the same job the only way of discerning between them is in terms of transfer speed. In other words how quickly can they translate your data into audio tones and audio tones back into data.

That speed is measured in terms of baud (bits of information per second). Only a few years ago 300 baud was considered the norm but today anything less than 14400 would be considered too slow. Indeed a 14400 BPS (14.4Kbps) modem will only be acceptable if you switch off the graphics when viewing sites. But since the graphical content of the WWW makes it what it is, switching off the 'pictures' rather defeats the object of surfing it in the first place!

If you are serious about surfing you have got to look at a 28.8Kbps speed modem at least, and preferably a 33.6Kbps. This will give you a good speed of access to other people's sites and also allow you to upload your own pages as and when you are ready to make your own contribution to the Web.

You should be able to get hold of a 28.8 Kbps modem for around £50 and a 33.6Kbps external modem for around £80 - £100. This price should include a UART chip which will be required by your computer to support transfer rates of 28.8Kbps or greater.

Several new modems claim connection rates of up to 56Kbps. However, tests on these devices show they fall well short of this most of the time.   Also, there are still some questions to be answered on communications standards.

Of course it is no use having a high speed modem if your access provider has a slower modem at their end of the telephone line.   But you needn't worry about this since virtually all access providers have at least a 33.6Kbps modem access.   However it is still worth making a note to check that your Internet access provider does indeed have a high speed modem connection, before signing up.

Another reason for using a faster device is that a lot of ISPs **charge you per hour** of access.   Even if they charge a flat fee, you will be 'on the phone' for the duration of your surfing session, incurring phone company charges.   So the quicker you can transfer and download your data, the less time you will be on-line, and the lower your costs will be at the end of the day.

You should also make sure that the modem you are intending to buy is **BT approved**.   While this is a requirement for all modems to be connected to the telephone line, occasional foreign, non-BT-approved modems do slip into the country, and these should not be connected to the telephone network.   Look on the back of the modem for a sticker of approval to make sure.

You may also wish to buy a fax modem.   These modems allow you to send faxes to and from your computer as well as creating normal links onto the Internet.   Of course, it is irrelevant as far as Internet usage goes, but it is still a sensible investment and helps you further down the way towards a paperless existence.

Ensure that the modem you are about to buy comes with all the necessary **cables** for connecting to your computer and the telephone line. And look for offers of free software.

Installing a modem is virtually painless if you are running Windows 95, Windows NT or using a Mac.   But if you are still on Windows 3.1 you could run into problems due to 'port conflict' (when two accessories try to use the same connection).

Solving these problems is well beyond the scope of this publication, and beyond most people to be fair.   If it happens to you, your best bet is to find someone who has already been through it themselves, buy a load of beer, and invite them round for the evening.

Telephone Lines

For most users a **standard** BT or Mercury telephone line should be sufficient.

Other lines do exist such as ISDN lines (Integrated Services Digital Network) but these should only be needed if you are intending to set up your own server.

Myth: It costs a lot to surf.

Truth: Only if you call £9 per month expensive. But how do you value your time - more than 6p per hour? And how much do those 20 'useful' channels cost on cable or satellite?

Software

The exact software that you need will depend very much on what sort of computer you have, which access provider you are using, and which services you are intending to use on the Internet.

Commercial packages are advertised and are easily available. However I would recommend that you wait and use the software that is usually **provided from ISPs** before splashing out.

At least that way you will get to find out which functions are necessary and which are just nice add-ons. Why, for example, get all singing, all dancing, browser software that will allow you to author all web pages when all that you want to do is surf an hour a week?

Even once you have decided that you need some of the less common functions found on Internet software you may find that your ISP has a deal. Software manufacturers often allow access providers to offer their products direct to you at a reduced cost.

Internet Service Providers

The term ISP stands for Internet Service Providers but we will tend to call them access providers in the rest of this publication since the term 'service' can mean anything in this day and age.

TIP

Try calling your intended access provider's technical support line at different times of the day and night and find out how quickly it is answered, if it is answered at all.

SLIP/PPP

SLIP/PPP accounts require special software from your access provider. However this form of connection allows your computer to actually join the Internet and talk the same language as the rest of the Internet. So, for the duration of your connection to the Internet, SLIP/PPP (Serial Line Internet Protocol/Point-to-Point) allows you to become, in effect, a mini host on the Internet.

The principal benefit of such a connection is that you are now talking the same language so everything you do on the WWW will be recognised by the other computers. If you downloaded any form of SLIP/PPP compatible software from the Internet it will allow you to use those services whether or not you pay your access provider for them.

Finding an Access Provider

As you will realise by now an access provider or ISP is essential for your connection to the WWW, and they fall roughly into two categories; those with a '**back bone**' and those without.

Back bone access providers usually have dedicated, permanent high-volume connection up and down the country. They are hard wired into the Internet providing access 24 hours a day, 7 days a week, 52 weeks of the year. There isn't much that happens on the Internet without them knowing since they are an integral part of it. Generally speaking, back bone providers are more reliable than those without a back bone.

Access providers without a back bone may be able to provide you with a cheaper connection though this is not always the case. That is because they tap into somebody else's back bone and offer you a service in a different manner. What is more, non-back bone providers may not have access to the entire back bone of the access provider on which they are piggy backing,

But that all sounds like jargon. What does it really mean to you? Well, back bone providers will usually be able to offer you a **POP**, or a point-of-presence, which is closer to your home than non-back bone providers. A POP is a server computer which you dial into in order to connect to the Internet. For example, it is no good having a service provider whose main computers are based in London if you are resident in the Shetlands.

So access providers particularly those with a back bone, set up POPs around the country to enable you to make a cheaper call. What is the point of having a global low-cost communications network if you have to make long distance phone calls to become part of it. So one of the most vital aspects of finding an access provider is to find one with a POP which allows you to make a low-cost local call.

Reader Offer

Because its an ideal way to get started and this is the **Complete Beginners Guide to the World Wide Web** on the Internet, we have teamed up with CompuServe to bring a special **free reader offer**. By sending off the coupon at the back of this book you will be able to connect to CompuServe's information services and start surfing the Web immediately. Turn to page 108 to find out how you can obtain your:

● Free Internet software **including a Web browser**

● Free access to the Internet for 10 hours

● Free CompuServe Information Manager software

● Free access to CompuServe for 1 month

● Free subscription to the bi-monthly Go magazine, and

● Free space on the World Wide Web

You may also come across the term virtual point of presence (**VPOP**s). This is simply a way of allowing you to make a local phone call and then diverting your call to a regular point of presence. It is simply a phone call diverter.

Most access providers will give you the information required to find out if they have a point of presence near your home or your business. But if you are unsure of the information you are given or want to make your own decision you can simply refer to your phone book. Here you will find the STD codes for all the towns and cities within your local call area.

Charges

In recent years the number of access providers has ballooned thus pushing down their charges. You should look out for a small start up charge and usually a monthly or annual subscription.

The start up charge will be in the range of £25 to £50 and the annual charge can vary from around £50 up to £300 per annum. However, as we have indicated, these prices are in a state of flux though it should not be long before a base price is reached.

It's as true of the Internet as it is with everything else, that you get what you pay for. For example you may be able to find an access provider that has no start up costs and which maybe only charges you £5 to £10 per month.

But it is no good having this brilliant access provider if you can never get on to their machine and access to the Internet in the first place. **This is particularly important if you are going to Surf at weekends and in the evenings.** Most people access the WWW during these times and you may find all the lines into the access providers computers are in use. In which case all you'll get is an annoying **engaged** or line-busy signal. If in doubt, ask around and find someone who already uses the provider you are looking at and ask them if they ever experience problems. Also read one or two or the monthly Internet magazines which carry connection statistics.

Other things to watch out for are time based charges. Company A may charge more than Company B as an annual subscription but may give you limitless access to the Internet. Whereas Company B charges less per year but adds a small extra rate of £1 or £2 per hour. You will find these time charges will soon add up and make Company B more expensive.

Most access providers gives you software for connection to their machines but you should still ask to make sure. Whilst you are asking, find out if they have a licence to distribute the software or whether it is shareware for which you may have to pay a registration fee later.

Technical Support

One of the major factors that you should consider when deciding on an access provider is the amount of technical support they will give you. Obviously in the early days it is extremely important that you can get on the WWW and stay there with a minimum of fuss.

You will find that the quality of technical support varies quite drastically. Some access providers give you a very poor or non-existent service, whilst others are excellent and answer every phone call within seconds. Ask about the particular kind of support that is going to be available and when it will be available. If you are simply going to access the WWW and use it mainly in the evenings during cheap rate it is no good having technical support that is open from 9 to 5pm.

Free Space

Sooner or later you are going to want to put something on the Web yourself - your own pages. To do this you either need a computer of your own permanently connected to the Internet, or you will need space on someone else's. Recognising this desire, most access providers now give a limited amount of **free space** while you are signed up with them.

From their point of view it will encourage you to stay put, since changing provider will entail you moving your pages and hence changing the address. Note, however, that most providers do not allow you to use your free space for commercial activities - so it's no good if you plan selling something over the Web.

Access Provider Check List

☐   Is local access available?

☐   Is there a one off start up charge?

☐   What is the monthly/annual charge?

☐   Is there an hourly rate?

☐   What services are available? Is there just Email and News groups or do they allow the full range of access including World Wide Web?

☐   Do they have dedicated technical support and what times is it available?

☐   How much information will they allow you to store on their machine?

☐   Do they provide free software, and is it licensed or share ware?

☐   Do they give you free web publishing space, and if so, how much?

☐   Is it a back bone or non back bone provider.

Have modem will travel

As you will see there are no right ways of joining the WWW but there are plenty of wrong ways, and it is unlikely that you will get it correct first time. It is only by using the Web and gaining experience that you are going to find the right service for you.

Don't worry though, because you have got a modem it is easy to swap between access providers so long as you do not get talked into a cheap, low-rate deal which is for a minimum period of a year or so. The biggest weapon you have in your armoury against being ripped off by an ISP is to increase your knowledge about the WWW.

Chapter 2

Domain Name System

THE INTERNET is made up of hundreds of thousands of computers all linked together for the purpose of communicating with one another. These computers may be in their own local area network which is then connected to the Internet, or they may be connected to the Internet directly. Obviously with so many computers wanting to talk to one another they need to be given names and addresses - just like humans. For example, if you wanted to send somebody a letter you first put on the envelope their name followed by their address, the town they live in and then their post code. And so it is with computers except they prefer to use numbers instead of letters.

These numerical addresses are stored in a collection of large databases which individual computers then consult in order to locate the specific computer with which they wish to communicate. So the Domain Name System (DNS) is essentially like a giant map splitting the Internet into areas, cities, streets and individual houses.

Everytime you go onto the World Wide Web your computer will need to use the DNS to find the pages you wish to look at. Don't worry, however, because **it is not necessary for you to understand the DNS** for reasons which we will come onto later. You should, however, be aware of what is going on so that you won't be totally confused when your computer produces an error message because it has failed to find the site you asked for.

IP Addresses

Every computer that is permanently linked to the Internet is given an Internet Protocol Address (or IP Address) so the other computers can find it in the DNS. These addresses consist of a 32-bit number sequence made up of four 8-bit numbers. Each of these 8-bit numbers are in the range 0-255 and the four sets are separated by full stops.

A typical IP Address may look like this:

123.255.7.193,

or

140.69.4.231

Your computer will also be allocated an

WHAT IF THE COMPANY YOU KEPT WASN'T YOURS?

CHECK NO ONE ELSE OWNS YOUR DOMAIN NAME NOW

NetNames, the International Domain Name Registry

Now from £79 per Name

For a limited period NetNames UK is reducing its single name fee to only £99 (costs differ for overseas registrations), with discounts for multiple registrations. The new pricing still covers all our FREE services and ensures that NetNames provides the best Domain Name registration service worldwide. Call FREEPHONE 0800 269049 (UK) to take advantage of this offer and ask about our further discounts for multiple orders.

Special Offer

Register a Domain Name with NetNames and obtain the new .tm name for only £49 (usually £99) + £35 (1 year's local fee). Register 5 or more names in one order, and obtain one .tm name completetly free (includes 1 year's local fee).

NetNames registers domain names for a fee
http://netnames.co.uk

info.
- Corporate Services
- NameQuestions
- NameNews
- About NetNames

ordering
- order your name now
- or freephone 0800 269049 (UK)
- Filing Requirements

search
- [Search]
- .co.uk & .com

IP Address when you get full Internet access. If you are using a Point-to-Point Protocol connection (PPP) your host computer will allocate a new address everytime you log on. Otherwise you will be using a Serial Line Internet Protocol (SLIP) connection and you will get a fixed address.

Have you got that? Good. Now you can immediately forget it all again. **Because you are unlikely to ever see IP Addresses referred to like this**. It is a plain fact of life that people are not as good at remembering sequences of numbers as computers are. Instead we prefer to use names and words.

Naming Domains

Along side the numerical IP Addresses computers are also given more recognisable names in plain English, like:

net-works.co.uk

which is a lot easier to remember. You can see how this is fairly similar to the numerical IP Address in that the different sections of the "English" address are separated by full stops (usually pronounced "**dot**"). The **.uk** part of the address tells you that the computer is in the United Kingdom; the **.co** tells you that the computer belongs to a company; and the **net-works** tells you which company's computer you are looking for.

These "English" addresses are stored along side the IP Addresses in the DNS. This is so the computers can still use the numerical sequences as their preferred way of referring to one another, and then use the English names as a way of communicating the information back to us.

So the sequence of events is something like this. You type in a Domain address such as **net-works.co.uk** and your computer immediately refers to the Domain Name System database via a link to the Internet. From the database it finds the 32-bit numerical address it requires and uses a standard protocol known as TCP/IP (Transmission Control Protocol/Internet Protocol) language to find and talk to the computer you requested. If you then ask for some information from the person or company at the other end they will ask you for your address which you will naturally type in English. Their computer will then use a similar process to look up your address in the DNS so their computer can talk to yours.

Interpreting Domain Names

Take the Domain previously mentioned:

net-works.co.uk

This indicated a computer, or some disk space on a computer, assigned to the company "net-works" (actually Net.Works but the 'dot' obviously can't be used) who are situated in the United Kingdom. If that company had been located in France then the final two letters of the name would have been **.fr**. So the new Domain Name would have been:

net-works.co.fr

Similarly if it had been located in Japan the last two letters would be **.jp** and the address would become:

net-works.co.jp

If the company net-works is a non-profit organisation then it would have been given the letters **.org** instead of .co. So its Domain Address would have been

net-works.org.uk

...and if it had been part of the Government you would have the letters **.gov** to become

net-works.gov.uk

These identifiers are known as Top Level Domains and those currently supported by the group which looks after these things are:

Name	Description	Name	Description
com/co	Commercial organisations	gov	Non-military government organisations
edu/ac	Educational institutions (universities etc.)	mil	Military government organisations
		int	International organisations
org	Non-profit organisations	uk	Two-letter (ISO) country codes, such as fr & au; uk is United Kingdom. There are more than 250 of these.
net	Networks (usually connected via a gateway)		

Look out for newcomers on the block. New top level domains on the cards include:

firm	Businesses or firms
store	Businesses selling products
web	Sites related to the WWW
arts	Sites for cultural and entertainment activities
rec	Recreation and entertainment sites
info	For sites offering information services
nom	For personal home pages

The .uk section of the domain name is referred to as the **Country Code**, and the .co section is the **Top Level Domain**. Then the "net-works" description refers to the **Second-Level domain** name and is usually assigned to an organisation of some sort. So, net-works.co.uk is a second-level domain of the .co and .uk Top Level Domains.

You will see a similar construction for a second level domain of your Internet service provider. The domain **demon.co.uk** refers to a computer in the United Kingdom belonging to an organisation called Demon. In this instance however the organisation (Demon) has a large Internet presence and may have several computers connected to the Internet.

Each of these computers will be given a distinct name which is added to the front of the domain name. So a computer known as bluebird and belonging to the organisation Demon would have the domain name **bluebird.demon.co.uk**. There may be several of these computers each with a different name but they will all be part of one site with the domain name of demon.co.uk.

URL

URL is short for **Uniform Resource Locator** and it allows you to specify an exact page on the World Wide Web. For example the URL:

http://www.net-works.co.uk/books/experts.htm

consists of three main sections.

The protocol name (**http://**) indicates the way in which you are accessing the data. All pages accessed on the World Wide Web use the "http:" protocol name whereas a document accessed using File Transfer Protocol uses the "ftp:" protocol name. There are many other protocol names for various Internet access methods such as Gopher and Telnet and you can learn more about these in *The Complete Beginners Guide to the Internet* also published by Net.Works.

The domain name (www.net-works.co.uk) is the name of the computer or part of the computer used by the organisation net-works (the publishers Net.Works). The **www** indicates that the computer contains information which can be viewed on the World Wide Web. The resouce location (**/books/experts.htm**) indicates the exact location of a specific page on the net-works computer.

Just as you store information on your own computer in directories or folders so the information is stored on a World Wide Web Server Computer. So the above resource location indicates that you need to look in the sub-directory books to find a file called experts.htm. Your Browser will then be able to open this file and you will be able to read the information contained in it on your computer screen at home.

Some URLs, you will notice, may not give an exact resource location. For example,

http://net-works.co.uk/

In this case the Server will display a default page also referred to as the "home page" for the domain.

Accessing a URL

Whenever you see a URL, in a magazine, on the television or on a leaflet, you can access that information simply by typing it into your Browser and hitting the return button (more on exactly how in chapter 3).

Usually you won't need to type the "http://" section of the URL since your Browser will often take this as read. So to access Net.Work's home page you type www.net-works.co.uk and press the **enter** key.

At this point it is worth remembering that you are dealing with computers who are an extremely pedantic species. Even if you get the URL slightly wrong you will receive an error message. Points to note here are:

✘ don't leave any spaces when you type a URL. Spaces are not allowed in URL's and if you see one typed in print then it will be by accident

✔ Type the URL exactly as you see it making sure that you match lower and upper case letters exactly. Most, but not all, Servers won't let you access a document unless you match the capitalisation exactly.

✔ Look out for the extension on the resource location. Some World Wide Web documents have the extension .htm whilst others have the slightly longer version of .html - make sure you get the right one.

✔ Find the tilde (~) on your key board. The origin of the Internet is closely connected with UNIX computers and as a result many home directories begin with a tilde. This is not a mistake as at some point in your career you will need to type it.

The Good News

Chapter four will deal with navigating on the World Wide Web in more detail. However you will be pleased to hear that typing URL's is not very common. This is because the World Wide Web uses a system of **hyperlinks** to allow you to navigate around the system.

Simply by clicking on a linked word, sentence or graphic your computer will be instructed to search for a specific URL linked to that word, sentence or graphic.

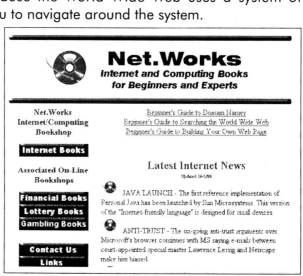

Chapter 3

You and Your Browser

IN THE BEGINNING there was one decent Browser known as "NCSA Mosaic". This was the software that revolutionised the Internet and started the upsurge in the popularity of the World Wide Web. Then half of the team that put the software together quit and started their own company. And so it was that "**Netscape**" was born. Since then the original team have found themselves several hundreds of millions of dollars better-off, and the company has grown hugely. Indeed it seems that hardly a month goes by without a new version of some Netscape Software being released.

But success breeds imitation and these days there are over 30 different Browsers you can choose from. Most of these are not even worth mentioning with the exception of one mighty contender to the Netscape crown - **Microsoft Internet Explorer**. Obviously Bill Gates and Co did not like being left behind by a group of upstarts, so they threw billions of dollars at the project and came up with their own Browser. Since most World Wide Web pages are created for one or other of these Browsers, beginners need not look much further in making their own choice. But more of that later.

Apart from allowing you to see the pages stored on other computers around the world, which form the World Wide Web, the main function of the Browser is to allow you to navigate between the different computers. The whole subject of navigation will be covered in the next chapter, so this section will concentrate on the "look and feel" of your Browser along with the other buttons and menu items which do not relate to navigation.

Installing and configuring your Browser is beyond this text and it is assumed that your Internet Service Provider's installation software will have installed it correctly so that it communicates with your dialer and you have no problems connecting to the Internet.

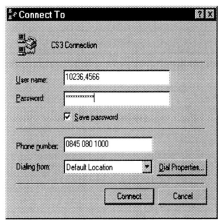

Logging on to the World Wide Web

Connecting to the World Wide Web with Microsoft Internet Explorer or Netscape is simplicity itself. Just select **Start, Programs, Netscape Navigator** or **Start, Programs, Internet Explorer**. Alternatively double click on your Explorer or Netscape shortcut icon. You will then see a "**connect to**" dialogue box which allows you to enter your username and password for connection to your Service Provider.

The same box also has a field for entering the phone number that you will dial to connect to your Provider. Usually you will not need to change this but if your Service Provider has more than one connection point and the one which you wish to use is busy, you could try typing in one of their other phone numbers and connecting to a different point of presence.

Once the connection procedure has been followed your Browser will display the **Default Start Page** that is configured within the Browser. Usually this will be the home page of the Company that has provided the Browser. For example, if you got Microsoft Explorer with your computer or your Windows 95 CD you will probably find that your default start page is Microsoft home page at *http://home.microsoft.com/* and if you receive Netscape it will be *http://home.netscape.com/*.

Another possibility is that your ISP has configured the Broswer to display their own home page when you first connect so you can see the latest news from your Provider and see what is happening on their server.

These default start pages can be a little annoying as they leave you with a feeling of being pushed into seeing what Microsoft, Netscape or your ISP will want you to see. Since everything you will look at will be your own personal choice, by typing in URL's or hitting hyperlinks, this procedure feels "unwanted". However the good news is that you can change this default start page to the one you prefer. I will show you how later.

Understanding the Screen

The illustration on page 25 shows the Microsoft home page as viewed with the Microsoft Internet Explorer Browser version 3.02. Since Internet Explorer is supplied free of charge on the CD that we are offering you with this book (see page 108) the following sections will describe features and elements of the Explorer Browser. However Netscape users will be able to follow this very easily since there is very little difference in the main features of both Browsers. This hardly surprising since both pieces of software are designed to do exactly the same job.

Title Bar

This shows you the "title" of the document you are currently looking. In the examples shown on page 15 the title is "Internet Start" and the title is set by the person who created the page (called the **webmaster**) before it was loaded onto the computer connected to the World Wide Web.

Menu Bar

These are drop down menu's for your Browser's main commands.

Tool Bar

These are graphical buttons which can be pressed with the click of your mouse and show the most often used commands available on the Browser.

Address Box

This is where you type in the URL of a Web page that you wish to visit and if you have been using hyperlinks it will show the current Web address of the document you are looking at. Although it is called *"**address**"* in Internet Explorer you may find that it is called *"**location**"* or *"**net site**"* in Netscape Navigator. Click on the arrow at the right of the address box to see a drop down menu showing a list of the pages you visited recently.

Links

These are called **directory buttons** in Netscape Navigator or **links** in Internet Explorer. Click on the links button to see a new set of buttons which will connect you directly to special Web pages. In Netscape Navigator you will find these directory buttons lead you

Understanding the Web Browser Screen

Program Icon ————

Title Bar ————

Menu Bar ————

Toolbar ————

Address ————
Box

Directory ————
Buttons
(view by
clicking)

Scroll Bars ————

Status Bar ————

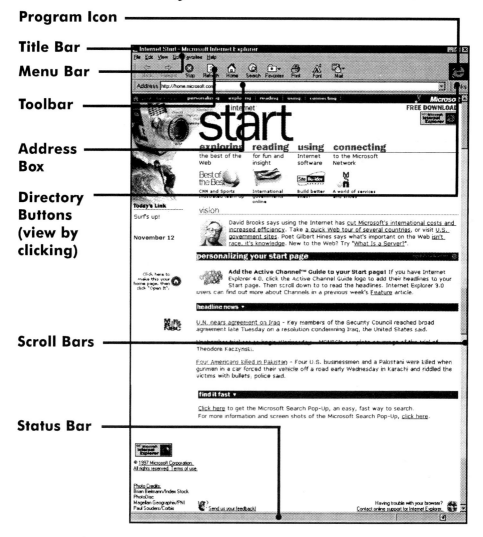

to pages showing you what is new on the Web, what are "cool" destinations, a search page, people and software.

Whereas Internet Explorer gives you different names for the same thing with best of the Web, today's links, a Web gallery, product news and, of course, a link to Microsoft. Here Internet Explorer has an advantage over Netscape in that you can customise the directory buttons to your own preferences.

Program Icon

When this icon is moving, or is "animated", the Browser is downloading information from the World Wide Web.

Scroll Bars

These bars will appear when a document is wider or longer than your window size. As with all other programs click the **scroll** arrow to move in the direction indicated. You can also drag the boxes along the scroll bar or click to the right or left (above or below) the boxes.

Status Bar

This gives you **information** about what your Browser is doing and varies considerably between Internet Explorer and Netscape.

The Tool Bar

As indicated above, the main items on the Tool Bar are for navigating around the World Wide Web. There are some interesting buttons you should be aware of:

Stop

Quite simply stops your Browser downloading information from the World Wide Web. This may be because it is taking too long and you are bored, or you have made a mistake in the URL that you have typed. You will also have to hit the stop button sometimes before your Browser will allow you to go forwards or back in your work.

Refresh

This will get you a new copy of a document you are wishing to look at.

This may sound a bit daft - what is the use in getting another copy of something you have just looked at? But you are underestimating your computer's ability to put words in your mouth!

When you type in the URL of a site that you have already visited the information that your Browser needs may still be stored in the "**cache**" on your computer. In which case the Browser will automatically load the information from the cache instead of downloading it from the Web, which will take longer.

For example, say one of your favourite pictures on the World Wide Web displays a new painting every week. That painting will enter your Browser as an image file with a name something like *painting.gif* or *painting.jpg*. So next time you try to connect to that Web page your computer will search for an image file called *painting.gif* and will find it in the cache to load it directly onto your screen. In this situation you would hit the refresh button so that the Browser is forced to connect to the Web site again and will download the new *painting.gif* that you wish to view.

A handy hint is also to use this button when a page has taken a particularly long time to download. Try hitting the stop button and then the refresh button and quite often you will find that the page will load quicker than it was doing before.

Favourites

Also know as **bookmarks**. This is a stored list of your favourite Web sites and will be covered in more detail later in this chapter.

Print

Clicking on this button will send the current page that you are viewing to your printer.

Fonts

This allows you to change the display font as seen on your screen

Mail

This allows you to access your E-mail within your Web Browser.

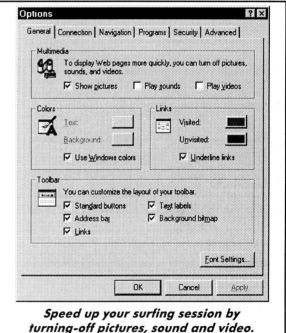

Speed up your surfing session by turning-off pictures, sound and video.

More Things You Can Do With Your Browser

One of the main drawbacks of the World Wide Web is perhaps its strongest points - its graphical richness. Sometimes, when Web usage is high, it can take a long time to download images for a page which you wish to look at. So you can speed things up by taking the option of not downloading images.

In Internet Explorer go to the command **view** and select the bottom command **options**. Now click on the tag **general** and you will see that the top box gives you multimedia options. To display Web pages more quickly, turn off the pictures by removing the tick from the **show pictures**. Note that you can choose whether to hear sounds or play videos by checking or unchecking the adjacent boxes.

In Netscape Manager go to the **Options** command and uncheck the **auto load images** command which appears on the drop down menu.

Once you have had a look at the page without the images you may decide that you would like to look at them so simply click on the images individually or choose "load images" from the menu.

News and E-Mail

As Browsers get more sophisticated they are giving you more and more options that do not really have anything to do with the World Wide Web. You may already know you can send and receive e-mail through your Browser but you can also connect to new servers and view the messages in the newsgroups on the GUI Interface. You will need to contact your ISP to find out how to configure your Browser to form these tasks.

Right Mouse Button

Both Netscape and Microsoft Internet Explorer make use of the right button on your mouse to give you a list of the most useful commands wherever you are on the World Wide Web, by holding down the right mouse button to see what is available. Some examples include "forward", "back" and "save link as", etc.

Copying Text

You can copy text from Web pages just like you would from any other document. Simply highlight the section that you wish to copy and choose "copy" from the edit menu and paste it into any text editor such as a word processor or an e-mail program.

Saving Pages

Saving a page as a bookmark or a favourite simply puts a link in your Browser so that you can go back to the page next time you are on-line. If you want to **read it off-line**, particularly useful if there is a lot of text, you may want to save it to disk. Go to the **file menu**, choose **save as** and you will be given the option to save the pages in **html** (Web) page or as **text**.

Selecting html allows you to view the page with your Browser again going to the file menu and selecting "local file". Saving the page as a simple text file will remove all the hypertext tags so that you can read it using the word processor.

Viewing the Source

Once you have been around the World Wide Web for a while you may be interested in putting your own pages up on the Web. The good way to start this off is to look and see how other pages have been created. You do this by looking at the "document source" which can be selected by going to the **view** menu and clicking on **document source**. You will be able to see how different Web authors use features such as "meta tags" and "frames" to enhance their Web sites.

Plug In's

P lug-In's are handy little pro-grams that work in conjunction with your Browser to perform a particular function.

They vary in the way they work slightly between Netscape Navigator and Microsoft Internet Explorer mostly as a result of the way in which the Browser manufacturer sees the World Wide Web heading.

Netscape Navigator believes that it has become so central to the way that you work on the World Wide Web that it is almost like an operating system in itself. So they allow other software manufacturers to make "Plug-ins" that you start up from inside the Browser.

Microsoft, however, see the Internet Explorer as just another application which runs with the Windows 95 Explorer. The Plug-ins therefore start under Windows 95 Explorer as opposed to the Internet Explorer. This way you are only running one operating system at a time and can jump between applications at will. In essence you will treating the World Wide Web as just another disk drive on your computer.

There are literally hundreds of Plug-in's to do such things with your Browser as play real audio live music, deliver real time stock exchange information, read spread sheets, view fractals, and display virtual reality worlds.

How much you will need any of these Plug-ins is open to debate and your own preferences but here are the Plug-ins that you would be well advised to lay your hands on:

RealAudio 2.0

This allows you to hear live sounds such as music, interviews and news if you have a sound card on your computer. You can obtain a copy from:

www.realaudio.com/products/ player/download.html

Shock Wave

This is used for MacroMedia Director animations and can be downloaded from:

www.macromedia.com/ shockwave/download/ index.cgi

QuickTime Virtual Reality

This gives you access to more than 80% of the multimedia content on the Web and to play QuickTime movies:

http://quicktime.apple.com/ sw/sw.html

Adobe Acrobat Reader

This Plug-in allows you to view Adobe Acrobat files and print out pages laid out as in a printed magazine. Get your reader from:

http://www.adobe.com/ prodindex/acrobat/main.html

Lightening Strike

This is a very good quality image compressor particularly useful if your hard disk is getting full. Go to:

http://www.infinop.com/ fhtml/entrypt.html

Add To Favorites...
Organize Favorites...

1997 UK National Lottery Winning Num...
Banners
Bookshop Search Page
Casino Gambling - Home Page from The...
Competitions
LATEST Lottery NEWS
Lottery and Lotto Products
NASA Images
Reuters - Shell Transport & Trading Co P...
RUNNERS-UP
Search engines
Shares
Ski Instructor Links
SnowPro - CSIA - CSCF - CASI
UK National Lottery Winning Numbers
WebCrawler Add URL
Welcome to The World of Gambling
Yahoo!

Bookmarks for the month as sorted by Internet Explorer - not easy to 'scan' with the eye very quickly

Bookmarks

Whenever you find a page on the World Wide Web that you think you would like to pay another visit to you can save its location by adding it to your **bookmarks** or **favourites**. Simply go to the menu bar or tool bar select "favourites" (or "bookmarks") and then click on "add".

Now, every time that you are on the World Wide Web, you can go back to the favourites bookmark and simply click on the title of the page that you would like to visit. This will immediately open the page using your Browser and allow you to view the latest contents.

Pretty soon, however, you will find that your favourites folder may become so full of your favourite sites that it is very near useless. Just take a look at some of the favourites I have collected in the last month at the bottom left of this page. They are auto-matically sorted into alphabetical order based on the first letter of my description.

Favourite bookmarks sorted into logical folders

So if I click on favourites and try to find the latest price for my Shell shares (and I may want to do this quickly if the markets are crash-ing) I would probably have to scan the list two or three times to realise where I have saved it. Not very useful.

It would make sense therefore if I were to organise these favourites into sub folders to give more accurate descriptions. And the good news is that with both Netscape and Internet Explorer this is a relatively easy task.

The first thing to do is to decide how you are going to organise your favourite sites. Look at the sites you have already saved and try and think of a way of categorising them. Looking at my bookmarks you will see that these fall roughly into five different types of site; Lotteries, books, search engines, shares, skiing.

Apart from telling you something about my fragile psyche this gives an indication of useful titles of the sub menus that I should place these favourite places into. So that is exactly what I will do! This routine is based around Microsoft Internet Explorer but it is pretty much the same for Netscape. Go to the **save** and click on it. Then select **organise favourites**. You will be presented with a new win-dow which looks very much like a window created by clicking on "My Computer" on the desk top.

You will see that all your favourites are presented here in the same manner that files are displayed in "My Computer". Now either press your right mouse button and select **new** then **folder** and type in the name of the sub folder that you would like to create, or go to the tool bar at the top and click on the **new folder icon**. This will create new folders in very much the same manner as you create new folders on your hard drive.

Now comes the task of putting your favourite pages into these sub folders. By far the easiest way to do this is to **drag and drop** them. Select one of the pages with your mouse and simply drag it over the top of the folder that you have just created. It will disappear from the view you are looking at and you will find that it is now located in your sub menu of your favourites folder. Alternatively you can use the Shift+Delete and Insert buttons or Ctrl+X and Ctrl+V to perform the same task.

Changing the Starting Page

The creators of your Browser or your Internet Service Provider want you to go to their page on the World Wide Web in order to get some free marketing. So they will have inserted their URL in the default start page of your Browser. Unless you have got some strange behavioural disorder, in which case you may want this information, it is probably better to change your start page so that it is actually useful.

Do this by going to the menu bar and selecting **views**. Then click on **Options** followed by the **Navigation** tab. You will be presented with a screen which looks like that shown above.

In the **page list** box use choose **start page** if it is not already selected. Then in the **address box** carefully type the URL where you would like to start and don't forget to leave in the "http:/" part of the address.

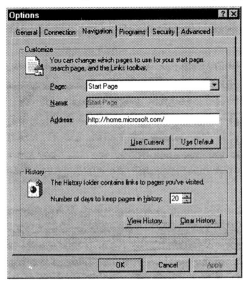

Changing the default start page

If, for example, you make heavy use of search engines you may want to start your Browser in a search engine as a way of kicking off your surfing. So in this situation you may insert the URL:

http://www.yahoo.com/

To start your surfing in the Yahoo search engine. Click "OK" and you are on your way.

Internet Explorer v Netscape

You should get the idea by now that Netscape and the Internet Explorer are very similar. This is because they have both designed to do the same job on the same World Wide Web.

There are, however, a few small differences between the programs which could lead you to choose one over the other.

Construction

Unless you are a programmer there is no difference between the way in which Explorer and Navigator look at pages. Both support the latest standards in programming specifications.

Speed

Both Explorer and Navigator are extremely fast compared to any other Browsers. It is achieved by caching and nice pieces of code such as just-in-time Java compilers. All things being equal Explorer has a slight speed advantage over Navigator, but the difference is very small. Your choice of modem and Internet Service Provider will have a far larger effect on the speed of viewing than your choice of Browser.

Downloading

Navigator has the edge here by showing the location of the files that you are downloading along with the name and the size of the file, a status bar and the percentage of the file already downloaded. On top of that it gives an estimate of the time remaining to download the whole file.

Explorer, on the other hand, throws up a silly little flying-files animation and gives you an indication of the number of bytes that it has downloaded already (plus an estimated download time). This is hardly as much use as the information provided by Navigator.

Looks

There is not a lot in it but Explorer gets a slight edge over Netscape in this category. Instead of square buttons that slightly depress when you click them as in Netscape, Explorer has a neat bitmap background and shows buttons which turn from monochrome to colour when your mouse hovers over the top of them.

Security

Both Browsers are packed with the latest versions of the security standard called **Secure Socket Layer** (SSL). Both also use certificates to allow you to tell a distant server that it really is you that is trying to gain access. It is also a way of telling you that you have connected to the site you intended and not one that some clever hacker has diverted you to. Honours are even in this category.

Controls

Neither Navigator nor Explorer get it right here. Explorer gives you password protection on the sites which adopt the Recreational Software Advisory Councils rating scheme (RSAC) but this is a voluntary self-censorship scheme which does not cover all sites on the World Wide Web by a long chalk.

Netscape goes far too far and gives you password protection to the whole of Navigator. Not exactly selective!

Requirements

Explorer requires a round about 8MB of ram to run efficiently and 4MB of disk space. Navigator on the other hand will require the same amount of RAM and needs up to 9MB of disk space when run under Win 95 and NT.

Summary

It is all horses for courses but **Microsoft Internet Explorer seems to have the slight edge over Netscape Navigator** by a short head. Perhaps the main reason for this slight advantage is that Explorer has the same look and feel as Windows Explorer does which most users will be familiar with from running Windows 95.

The Complete Beginner's Guide to Windows 95

This book isn't for the sort of people who get all frisky at the thought of a new operating system. They're already running Windows 95 and have been since day one. As the title suggests, it is for beginners:

You can read *The Complete Beginner's Guide to Windows 95* **on the train, during your coffee break or while you sit in front of your PC.** By the end of each chapter you'll have learned useful skills in Windows 95.

By the time you reach the last page you may not get shivers up and down your spine whenever you think of Windows 95, but you'll be using your computer with confidence, working a little bit smarter and having more fun along the way.

Price: £4.95

The Complete Beginner's Guide to Windows 95 is a low-cost, easy to understand guide, specially designed for everyone who hates wading through hundreds of pages of information to find a simple answer.

Ordering information on page 112

Chapter 4

Navigating the WWW

THERE ARE literally tens of millions of pages of information on the World Wide Web, and each of these have a unique URL. So one of the most important things that you need to know is how to get around this plethora of information. It would be folly indeed just to dive in at the deep-end every time you go surfing and just thrash about until you find some information you are interested in. So one of the first things you need to know is how you get to certain places and, if need be, get back again.

Hyperlinks

When you look at just about any page on the World Wide Web you will notice that some of the words and phrases are underlined and probably in a different colour. These are called **hyperlinks** or simply **"links"**. Quite simply the creator of the page has embedded some code "underneath" these words which will allow you to go to another page on the Web which contains some more information on those words.

For example, if you came across the text:

"Faced with possible Government intervention, many on-line organisations are seeking to establish a universally accepted code of practice detailing how potentially objectionable material is dealt with"

If you were to click on the hyper-link "on-line organisations" your Browser would connect to a new page on the World Wide Web most probably detailing some of the on-line organisations involved in this initiative. Also, if you click on the link "code of practice" then you would expect to progress to a page which talks about this specific code of practice, or codes of practice in general.

Of course, not all underlined words or coloured text are hyperlinks. Other ways of telling if words are linked to other pages is to move your mouse pointer over the top of the text in question and see if it changes shape. If the pointer changes into the figure of a little hand then that is a signal that you can click on the link and move to a new page. You will also notice the status bar at the bottom of your Browser will display the address of the page that you would go to should you click on the link.

Links are not limited to text. The creator of the Web pages could cause almost any form of image to link you to another page. Usually these images will be in the shape of a button to make it obvious that you are connecting to another page. But it could be any form of picture, or even an area on a picture. Again, if you are not sure, try moving your mouse pointer over the top of the image and watch for it changing shape and the URL appearing on the status bar. Also try moving your mouse pointer around any particularly large images that you see, especially those on home pages. You may find that the image contains several links pending on the part of the image that you are looking at.

Forward and Back

Let's go for an imaginary surf. Say you connect to your Internet Service Provider and you change your Browser so that the default page is the Yahoo search engine. This page loads fairly quickly and you type into the main search section "cars" and hit the search button. Yahoo thinks about your request for a few tenths of a second and sends back a page of links and descriptions of pages that contain information on cars.

On this page you find some information on Mercedes Benz, a car which you have always fancied. Although you have not got enough cash you can always dream, so you click on the hyperlink and go to the home page for Mercedes Benz.

After looking down the home page you spot an image of a sporty-looking saloon and when your mouse goes over the top it goes into the shape of hand. So you click on the image and are sent to another page on the Mercedes Benz site which gives you a full description of all their saloons along with technical spec. At the bottom of this page are three words underlined separated by dots. One says home, one says team Mercedes and the other says dealerships. So you click on the latter and are sent to a page listing all the dealers in Mercedes Benz saloon cars.

Yahoo Search Page

|

Search results

|

Mercedes Benz Home Page

|

Saloon Cars

|

List of Dealers

Now at this point you find your dreaming is taking you a little far and you realise it is pointless even looking to see if there is a dealer in your area because you cannot even afford a Reliant Robin. However you would like to go back and have another look at the details on the saloons. But there isn't a link on the page of dealers that says saloons. So what do you do?

This is where the "back" button on your Browser comes in handy. It is represented by an arrow pointing from right to left and is usually situated on the left hand side of your button bar.

Click your mouse over the top of this button and your Browser will re-load the last page you were at, in this instance the page about saloons.

Click on it again and you will return to the Mercedes Benz home page. Another click would take you to the Yahoo search results for "cars" and a final click would take you back to the Yahoo initial search page.

At this point you are back at the beginning of your surfing session and there weren't any previous pages. So you will find that the back button on your Browser will become dimmed and it won't allow you to press it.

The "forwards" button works in much the same way and is represented by an arrow going from left to right, usually the second button on your button bar. As you might have guessed pressing this button takes you to the next page in the sequence that you have been looking at.

So if you are at the Mercedes Benz home page clicking on the forward button would now take you to the page on saloons. A second click on the forward button would take you to the dealership page. Of course, you must have previously been to these pages for the forward button to function. Once you have arrived at the dealership page the forward button will be dim and it is no longer selectable.

That's History

Since your Browser is able to take you forwards and backwards to the sites that you have been visiting you might be starting to get the idea that it is keeping a list - and you would be right. This list is known as the "history list" and it is stored on your computer's hard disk. It is quite simply a list of sites that you may have visited on the World Wide Web on your present session or recent sessions.

This is stored in the order that you visited them for the first time and provides a basis for navigation with the forwards and backwards button. Clicking on the back button will take you up the list while clicking on the forward button will take you down the list. At each point that you stop at in the list the relevant page will load into your Browser.

Once you have been surfing for a while you may decide that you would like to go back to a site that you last visited a few sessions or a couple of days ago. In this instance you can hit the back button as much

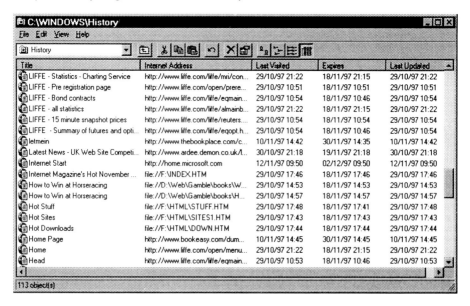

as you like but you will probably get nowhere near what you want. So you can shortcut the process by going direct to the history file.

Access this list in Internet Explorer by choosing **go** then **open history folder**. You will be presented with a window detailing all the sites that you have visited over a certain number of days. You will then be able to see:

- The title of the page
- It's URL or Web address
- The date you last visited
- When it "expires"
- When it was last updated

This is a particularly useful function in Internet Explorer as it allows you to sort the sites you have visited by any of the above categories. Clicking on the title bar will sort your sites from A-Z and clicking on it again will sort it from Z-A. Whilst clicking on the "last visited" bar will display all the sites in order from the site that you visited most recently to those that you visited a few days ago, or vice- versa. Simply double click on any of the sites to pay another visit.

You can control how many days that Explorer will keep the details of a particular page in its history list before it "expires". Specify the number of days by clicking on "view" then "options" and select the "Navigation" tab. Look at the history area of this screen and you will see an indication of the number of days before expiry. When an address "expires" it is automatically deleted from the hard disk.

If you are using Netscape Navigator you will find that the history list is not as good as that on Internet Explorer. It only lists the sites that you visited during the current session on the World Wide Web, which is a severe limitation. Open this list by choosing **window** and then **history** or press ctrl + H.

Can't Go Back

Occasionally you will come across a curious feature of the Browsers. You will be looking at a page on the Web and wish to go

Tip

If you are browsing sensitive information and you do not want anybody else to know which pages you have been visiting the history list can be a liability. Anybody else accessing your computer can go along to the history folder and see where you have been like foot prints in the snow. If you would like to cover your tracks click on "view" and then "options", and the "navigation tab". In the history area of this screen you will notice a button marked "clear history". Click on this and the evidence will be removed!

Mercedes Benz
Motor Racing
(side trip)

Yahoo Search Page

Search results

Mercedes Benz
Home Page

Saloon Cars

List of Dealers

back to one that you have recently visited. You know it was only a couple of
pages ago but no matter how hard you
search using the back and forward button you cannot find it.

This is not an error and your machine is not about to crash. It is actually
the Browser being very clever - trying to
speed up your session (though some
would say it is too clever). The history list is arranged so that it will ignore
none productive site trips on your searching sessions.

This is best illustrated by way of example. Remember you went on
an imaginary surfing session at the beginning of this chapter. Now say
you made a mistake along the way and ended up at a page that you
really did not want. You started with the Yahoo search page, entered
the phrase "cars" and received a page of search results.

Looking down this page you spot the word Mercedes and click on the
hyperlink. But instead of going to the Mercedes Benz production car
home page you find that you have located some information on the
Mercedes Benz racing team. You are not really interested in motor racing
so you hit the "back" button straight away.

This takes you back to the search results page find the correct link
and progress to the Mercedes Benz home page, followed by the saloons
and then the dealerships.

You will see that this surfing session is the same as the original apart
from the little "side trip" to the motor racing page. In this instance, starting from the dealerships page, you will click on the "back" button to go to
the saloons page and then to the Mercedes Benz home page.

Now you would expect another click on the "back" button to take
you to the racing page. But this does not happen. Another click of the
button will take you back to the Yahoo search result page for cars.
And when you go forwards again you will go back to the Mercedes
Benz home page.

The reason for this is that your Browser realised that you clicked on a link and then came straight back to the page it started from. So it assumes that you do not like the page you have been to and would never like to see it again. Most of the time this is very convenient, and the Browser designers have got it right - the page you visited was not of any use so you do not want to go there again. But there are odd occasions where you will visit a page and think "oh I will come back to that " and then exit using the "back" button. And that is the last you will ever see of it!

Site Navigation

A site on the World Wide Web is simply a collection of Web pages normally stored on the same computer and usually all concerned with the same subject or company.

For example, at the Mercedes Benz site you will expect to find pages relating to their cars, servicing, accessories, dealerships and everything relating to Mercedes Benz cars. So each page deals with a certain aspect of information and together they make up the "Web Site".

Another example would be *The World of Gambling* site which is found at the address:

www.gamble.co.uk

which has nearly 100 pages of information on gambling books, software and accessories. All of the pages are situated at the same site and on the same computer but they have different URL's.

When a company or individual creates a Web site they try to group all the information together in a logical structure, just as they would in a "real life" shop. And to help you "look around the shop" they put up various "signs" to help you navigate your way around. These are known as "internal navigation aids" and consist of links that the Web authors have included in the pages to help you find your way around.

These internal navigation aids are often presented as both links connected to images or buttons, and text-only versions of exactly the same links.

Why not take a look at the aforementioned *World of Gambling*

Tip

Even very experienced surfers of the World Wide Web do not realise that the history list excludes non-productive side trips. So you can impress people at parties and gain some street credibility by producing this nugget of information as a way of out-doing the local Internet bore.

pages by way of example? Enter the address:

www.gamble.co.uk

in the URL box of your Browser and hit return. You will find all the latest gambling news presented by *The World of Gambling*, and down the left hand side of the screen a series of buttons which give you links to gambling books, software, systems, accessories and games.

There are also links to pages where you can contact The World of Gambling, links related to gambling and FAQ's (frequently asked questions) also on the subject of gambling. However if you scroll to the bottom of the page you will see that there are also text links to the same pages.

Click on the "books" link and your Browser will load a page showing the top 10 gambling books distributed by the company and the book of the month.

This time, down the left there are a series of links to pages of books on particular gambling subjects. These are not the same links as you saw on the home page because the Web authors assume that, having got this far, you are interested in the books. Scroll to the bottom, however, and you will find text links similar to the ones that you saw on the home page just-in-case you would rather jump to another section.

Now, select any of the books in the top ten list. A page will load showing you details of the book you have chosen and down the left you will have text based links allowing you to jump to any of the other subjects in the gambling books section. There is also a link called "home" which will take you back to the top of the site, the home page for the company.

These links, inserted by webmasters, make moving around a particular site fairly easy and act like road signs. Once you are within a site if you were to use the back and forward buttons you will find that it is easy to become confused as to which direction you are heading in.

This is because the site is not built in linear fashion. In other words you do not enter at the home page and progress through a series of pages until you reach the end. It is more like a tree where you start at the base and move along the branches getting closer to some information but further away from others (see illustration above).

Frames

Web designers can divide a page into two or more independently scrollable windows called frames. They are useful in that it allows a designer to put a "table of contents" in one section of the screen and allows you to view the individual pages of information in the other frame. This allows you to jump around the site easier than otherwise possible by only using the contents panel to make your links.

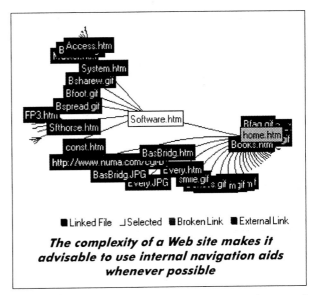

Linked File ⌐Selected ■Broken Link ■External Link

The complexity of a Web site makes it advisable to use internal navigation aids whenever possible

However they are not very popular with designers because of the variety of different Browsers that are available. Some Browsers support frames and others don't, and even if they do they can produce spurious results when you hit the back or forward buttons.

Try it for yourself. Find any site that uses frames and go two or three links into the site. Now try navigating around the site using the back and forward buttons. Perhaps everything will work as it should but you may find that the back button will always put you back to the home page or even throw you out of the site altogether.

Newer Browsers such as Internet Explorer or Netscape Navigator work with frames far better. However Web designers will take a while to be convinced that frames no longer confuse their visitors and start using them again.

Other Navigation Aids

By now you already have the basics to allow you to navigate your way around the World Wide Web. However there are a few more aids available to you.

The "Home" button. This is located on your button bar and will take you back to the Browser default starting page.

The "Search" button. This is also situated on the Browser's button bar for Internet Explorer users or the tool bar for Navigator users. It will load a page of search services.

Favourites/bookmarks. This was discussed in the previous chapter and gives you a quick way of jumping around the sites that you find most useful.

URL box. Don't forget that clicking on the arrow to the right of the URL box will display a selection of sites from your history list.

"Go" command. Clicking on the command to "Go" from your command line will open a drop down menu which will show a selection of addresses "intelligently" selected from your history list.

Starting page. Perhaps one of the most useful aids to navigating around the Web is where you choose to start off.

If you wanted to spend a week exploring the Scottish Highlands you would not choose a hotel in Birmingham as your base. Each day you would have to drive all the way up the M6 to before you even got close to the places you wanted to visit. Instead it would make more sense to base yourself in Edinburgh or Glasgow.

So carefully consider what you would like as a default start page in your Browser. If you look for a diverse array of information on a regular basis then a search engine makes a sensible place to start.

If, however, you are usually interested in one particular type of information such as investment data and only occasionally you look at other sites then you may wish your Browser to start at a page of investment information links.

It's Not There!

There are two main reasons why your attempt to locate and retrieve a page on the World Wide Web may fail. Firstly, and most commonly, the page you are trying to get has moved or never existed. Secondly, usually when you are starting on your surfing career, you have mis-typed or misunderstood the URL. Here are some of the more common errors:

File not found

If the file you are looking for has moved or changed its name then you will get this message which is known on the Web as a *"404"* after the error code that is produced for your Browser.

Apart from the page having moved (or never existed in the first place) make sure that:

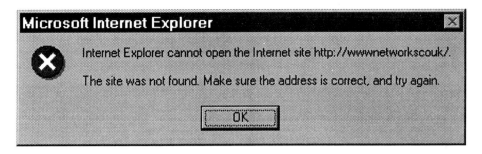

☐ You have matched the capital and lower cases exactly.

☐ You have not included spaces in the address, since these are not allowed in URL's.

☐ You have correctly typed any symbols such as the tilde and underscore correctly

☐ and you have got the right extension for the page e.g. html or htm?

Illegal Domain Name

If you go to an illegal host name then your Browser will give you this error message. The most common reason for this is that you have mis-typed the address. Each of these will give you an example:

Http//net-works.co.uk
http:/www.net-works.co.uk
http://www.networkscouk and
http://www.net-works.uk

Incorrect Host Name

This is when you are trying to access an address that does not exist and has no entry in the DNS.

Host Busy

With increasing regularity, due to the number of people joining the World Wide Web, the host serving the page you are trying to access will become overloaded.

This is because too many people are trying to access the page at the same time. It is usually a temporary error and it can be overcome by trying again later (in particular when the locals will be asleep - like accessing American sites during our morning).

Help Me

Y ou will be an extremely lucky person if you do not come across one or more of these errors every week. Indeed you may come across "file not found" by trying to access some of the pages recommended in this publication.

This isn't because we have given you the wrong address or mis-typed it (though that may have happened, because we are only human!) but because the World Wide Web is in a constant stage of flux.

Every day pages are being created, but also others disappear. Perhaps a company or person has a page on a certain ISP's computer, but they found a cheaper way to access the World Wide Web and changed ISP. So they have to take their page with them and load it onto another computer.

However there are a few tricks that you can try to see if the page really does not exist or that something is slightly wrong:

❑   Try changing the file name extension from ***.htm** to ***.html** and visa versa.

❑   Add or subtract the **www** at the beginning of the page address.

❑   Play around with the **capitalisation** of the address, but remember that host names are not case sensitive.

❑   Remove the last part of the file name so that you are just left with the **host name**. You can then follow links on the site to try and find the page that you require.

If all else fails take a few key words from the page you are trying to find and go to a search engine. Even if this still does not find the site that you require you will at least find similar sites and perhaps still get the information you are after.

Myth: The World Wide Web breaks down every couple of days.

Truth: There has only ever been one major breakdown of 'The Internet'. And that was for only four hours. When people say they, "can't get on the Web" they usually mean their ISP's server is busy or down - not the Net. Solution: find a more reliable ISP!

Chapter 5

Searching the Web

IT MAY BE hard to believe these days but there was a time when only a handful of Web sites were available on the World Wide Web. And this was not way back in ancient history but probably no more than 5-10 years ago. In those days regularl users had to memorise the addresses (URL) of the sites that they were interested in, if not all of the sites that were then available.

However this situation did not last for long and the number of Web sites started to blossom. As soon as there became more than about 50-100 sites it was obviously impossible to memorise or even keep a hand written record of all the addresses available.

The obvious solution to this was to keep a personal list of sites that you knew about on your own computer. In that manner you could keep track of all the URL's you could think of that were relevant to you, and then look at the list whenever you needed to find something. But what would happen if a new site came onto the World Wide Web and you knew nothing about it. It would not be in your list so you could not find it no matter how closely you scoured the results.

So friends and colleagues started exchanging lists and consulting one another's small databases of Web Sites. In this manner they got a better coverage of what was available and consequently a better chance of finding the information they required.

As with all things to do with computers there were a few individuals who took things to extreme. Two of these were University students called David Filo and Gerry Yang who started to make a catalogue of as many Web sites as they possibly could and put them into a database. They then created a Web site of all these listings and wrote the code to link each individual line of the list to the site itself. And so it was in 1994 that **Yahoo!** was born. This became the first Web directory and set the two creators on the path to a multi-million dollar fortune.

To start with, it was fairly unsophisticated and simply listed the sites under fairly broad category headings. But the boom in the number of Web sites caused the pair to sit down and figure out a more clever programming technique which would allow people to use their site and find what they wanted. Before long they came across search technology which allowed users to type in words or phrases at the top of the page and make a search of their database of Web sites.

Modern Search Engines

With a massive increase in the number of World Wide Web sites, today's search engines include an absolutely massive database at their core. These index complete lists of Web sites and information resources right across the Internet, and all of them aim to contain details on just about every Web site available.

Modern search engines fall essentially into three categories:

Passive search engines. These search engines are possibly more accurately referred to as directories. They rely on World Wide Web users to submit details of their site or their favourite sites in order to build up a database. Upon receiving the submissions somebody from the search engine company trots along to the Web site suggested has a look at it, and then places the details in the right part of the database by finding a main category and sub-categories into which the Web site should fall.

Active search engines. These engines rely on search programs known as "spiders" or "Web robots" to index and categorise Web pages as well as Web sites. The spider travels out into the World Wide Web in search of new sites and reports the results back to the search engine. It downloads all the information that the page contains and then examines that information to extract key words and phrases that can be used to categorise the site. The exact method that it uses to do this, and which information it looks at to create the index, varies according to search engine. Those

words and phrases are added to the database along side the URL and a description of the site.

Meta-search engine. This is a search engine that uses other search engines to give it the information. So when you type a word or phrase into a Meta-search engine it will consult with all the other directories and spider based search engines to gather a list of sites that you may be interested in.

Directories

The creators of Yahoo!, David Filo and Gerry Yang, may have started Yahoo! in their back bedrooms but in 1996 the company they created went public and raised over $800 million. This obviously gave them a huge amount of capital with which to improve the search engine. As a result they can now index over 1, 500 pages per day into their database. Yet you may be surprised to learn that even this rate does not keep up with the speed at which new pages are being added to the World Wide Web.

It has already been suggested as a site with which to start your surfing sessions, but you will find Yahoo! at:

Http://www.yahoo.com

Despite it's "age" this probably still the most important of search engines available on the Web. It is easy to use and has more useful links than you can think of.

Information is sorted into categories and sub-categories. There are seven main subject categories:

☺ art and humanities

☺ business and economy

☺ computers and Internet

☺ education

☺ entertainment

☺ government

☺ health

☺ news and media

☺ recreation and sports

☺ reference

☺ regional

☺ science

☺ social science

☺ society and culture

Each of these categories has many sub-categories and those sub-categories also contain their own sub-categories, and so on almost ad infinitum.

There are two main ways of using Yahoo. The first is to browse through the categories, and the second is to search the database.

Browsing Yahoo!

Finding information in Yahoo through browsing is probably best illustrated by way of example. Since you have bought this publication you are obviously interested in beginners guides to the World Wide Web. So trot along to the Yahoo home page and have a look at the main categories (mentioned above).

The obvious place for starting to look for information on the World Wide Web is in the main category heading "**Computers and Internet**". Indeed, listed underneath this main heading one of the sub-headings shown on the home page is "**WWW**". Double click on the hyperlink "Computers and Internet" to find the list of sub-categories. Since the World Wide Web is part of the Internet you would probably want to follow the links through the "**Internet**" link.

Once into this sub-category you will be presented with a lot of information on various parts of the Internet. There is everything from File Transfer Protocol to Gopher, and from Finger to Talk. The obvious category that you want to select is **World Wide Web**.

You now have another choice of sub-categories and sites themselves. But you are looking for a "beginners guide" and you are more likely to find this underneath **"information and documentation"**. Click on this hyperlink and load the next page.

You are now down to a sub-category of a sub-category of a main category within the Yahoo database. Your are almost there but not quite! You now need to look through the available categories and sites to decide what level of information you are after. The obvious choice here is **"beginners guides"**. click on this hyperlink and you will finally get through to a list of sites which are "supposed" to give you a beginners guide to the World Wide Web.

On the way through you should have noticed that categories and some **categories within Yahoo are always shown in bold**. These are easily distinguished from actual Web sites and pages which are shown in plain text.

Searching Yahoo!

Having gone through the almost exhaustive process of working your way through the subject tree of Yahoo with all its categories and sub-categories, etc you may wish there was a slightly easier way of finding information. There is. The Home page (and most other pages) gives you a search box. And perhaps the best way to learn how to use this facility is, again, by way of example.

Go back to Yahoo's home page either by clicking on the arrow to the right of the address box, by going to the "go" command, by selecting it from the history list, or by repeatedly hitting the "back" button. Obviously if you have set this page as a default start page in your Browser you have the option of clicking on the "home" button.

This time instead of clicking on the hyperlink "Computers and Internet" go to the top of the page and type "World Wide Web guide" into the search box. Then put your mouse over the top of the search button and click to initiate the engine. **Screen shot 1**.

Within a fraction of a second you will download a page similar to that shown in **screen shot 2**. You will see that Yahoo has found no less than five categories which satisfy your parameters and more than 200 sites or pages which are on the subject of World Wide Web guides. Looking down the list of categories you can immediately see that four of the

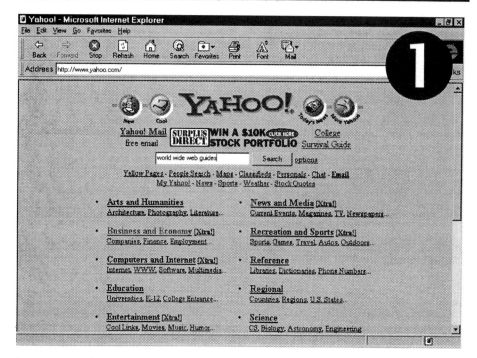

five are irrelevant. You are looking for a beginners guide so you will hardly be interested in research papers on the World Wide Web. You are looking for a guide to the World Wide Web itself and not a guide to events that are taking place on it, so the third category can be discarded. Similarly the last two categories deal with design and layout of pages on the World Wide Web and services of companies which can do this for you. These can also be discarded. So click on the second category:

Computers and Internet: World Wide Web:
Information and Documentation:
Beginners Guide

and you will receive back a page similar to that shown in **screen shot 3**. You will note at this point that you are only two pages away from the Yahoo home page. Compare this to browsing your way through the Yahoo subject tree of categories and sub-categories. By this point you would already be onto your fifth page.

Screen shot 3 now displays a list of sites which are supposed to contain the information that you are looking for. However you will see that several of them appear to have been misplaced. For example "*How to publish on the Web*" looks as if it would have been better off in the fourth category shown on screen shot 2.

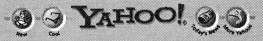

Yahoo! Search Results - Microsoft Internet Explorer

File Edit View Go Favorites Help

YAHOO! **2**

Yahoo! Mail - Yahoo! Chat with *Star Trek* cover girls Jeri Ryan and Terry Farrell

Categories - Sites - AltaVista Web Pages | Headlines | Net Events | Amazon.com Related Books

Found 5 Category and 204 Site Matches for world wide web guides

Yahoo! Category Matches (1 - 5 of 5)

Business and Economy: Companies: Books: Titles: Reference: Research Paper and the World Wide Web, The: A Writer's Guide

Computers and Internet: Internet: World Wide Web: Information and Documentation: Beginner's Guides

Computers and Internet: Internet: World Wide Web: Searching the Web: Web Directories: Event Guides

Computers and Internet: Internet: World Wide Web: Page Design and Layout: Beginner's Guides

Business and Economy: Companies: Internet Services: Web Services: Free Web Pages: Geocities: Guides

Yahoo! Site Matches (1 - 15 of 204)

Yahoo! - Computers and Internet:Internet.Worl... - Microsoft Internet Explorer

File Edit View Go Favorites Help

3

- FAQ - World Wide Web
- A Home Page on YOUR hard drive - Put a Home Page on Your computer to start your WEB surfing
- All About the World Wide Web
- Beginner's Guide To Life And The Internet - succinct and easily understood guide for Internet novices (written by a novice!)
- Burt's page of Internet Tips - Dedicated to Internet tips and interesting links.
- Creative Good: Help Pages
- Eric's Page - offers help with building Web pages.
- Exploring the World-Wide Web - self-directed tutorial for new web users.
- Finding a WWW Host for Your Project - Single page of suggestions on how to find a free/low-cost host for your WWW pages.
- Folksonline - for newcomers & non-technical folks. Inspirational stories, how-to articles, web tours all written by our community audience about their web experience.
- How to Publish on the Web
- ICYouSee Page - designed in connection with the Ithaca College Library Home Page to be a self guided World Wide Web training page.
- Internet 101
- Kitty Locker's Introduction to the Web - introduces university students to the Web, with links for research tools, designing web pages, job hunting, organizations, writers' resources, and more.
- Netman and Friends - help for new users and non-techies is here! Techno-babble is reduced to easy to understand English.
- Paging Yourself
- Sites to See - introduction to the Web.
- SquareOne - browsing, downloading, zip/unzip, FTP, e-mail, plug-ins and more. Subscribe to the free newsletter.

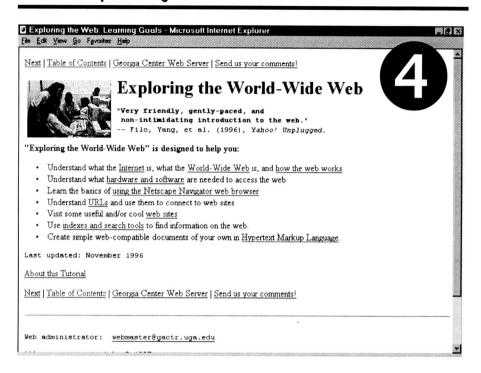

Nevertheless there is information here that you would be looking for. *"All about the World Wide Web"* looks interesting but there is no description to the right of it. Further down the list you will see a page titled *"Exploring the World Wide Web"* and it carries a description indicating that it is a self directing tutorial for new Web users.

This looks interesting so click on the hyperlink and you will discover a page similar to that shown in **screen shot 4**. Now you have reached the end of the line as far as the search engine goes. If you want to go any further you will be navigating within the site as described in the last chapter.

If the information shown on this page does not look as though it is of interest to you simply click on the "back" button to go back to screen shot 3 and select another site which may contain more relevant information.

You will notice that all the pages indicated on screen shot 3 have a title (most probably given by the Web site's creator) and brief description of the page. The down side of these descriptions are that they are entered by humans and could easily contain false information or exaggerations.

Too Many, Too Few

You will remember that at the level of screen shot 2 Yahoo had retrieved five subject categories and more than 200 sites that matched your search parameters. If you have been searching for a broader subject, something as simple as "Internet", or "computers", you could have retrieved tens of thousands of sites. Obviously there is no way that Yahoo can display all of those on one page so it will limit the number of results that it will put on one page.

If you look down the list and do not find anything that you require you will get to the bottom and one of the hyperlinks that you find there will direct you to the "**next 20 links**". Click on this link and Yahoo will deliver up another 20 possible matches to your search phrase. Again if you find nothing on this page at the bottom you will find another link labeled "next 20 links", and you will also find "**previous 20 links**" if you decide that you want to go back and have a look again.

Now even if you are a sad person who loves sitting behind your computer screen looking for one minute piece of information you will not be able to look through 10,000 Web sites without going mad. In this situation you are going to have to refine your search to cut down on the number of sites. In other words you are going to need to control how Yahoo is searching its database more closely.

Return to the Yahoo home page and next to the search box you will see a link simply titled "options". Click on this to find a screen shown on page 57. These options give you certain parameters which will help you refine the data that Yahoo finds in its database and deliver up more accurate listings.

Search by Date

When you start a search in Yahoo the engine automatically assumes that you want a look at all of those sites that it has ever categorised. In Yahoo terms this is over the last three years.

But on the options page you are able to select when the sites may have been added to the database. This is a way of cutting down on the amount of information that you receive back and make sure that you are finding only the most up-to-date material on the Web.

Click on the new listings box and you will see that Yahoo gives you the option of looking at sites that have been added during the past three years (the default), six months, three months, one month, one week, three days, and one day.

Boolean Searches

Using Boolean operators you can get Yahoo to retrieve any item that contains **ALL** of the words that you have typed or **ANY** of the words that you have typed. If you would like it to find sites that only contain all of the words then click on the "matches on all words (AND)". Should you want it to retrieve sites with any of the words that you have typed then click on the words "matches on any word (OR)".

Exact Phrase

If you were to go to the Yahoo search engine and enter the word "bad" into the search, the engine would retrieve pages which not only contain information on "bad" but also those on "badgers", pages relating to "badminton", and you may even come across some sites dedicated to "badges".

If you click on "exact phrase match" Yahoo will only find and deliver sites with exactly what you type. So searching on "bad" will retrieve sites with the word "bad" in their title.

Phrase

You can search on a phrase with as many words as you like simply by putting quotation marks at either end of the phrase.

Name

If you want to look for a person's name, say Roger Black, and do not want to retrieve sites which may be totally unrelated (for example on blackjack, black magic, or black politics) then make sure you select "a person's name" from the options available.

Search Area

Another useful way of limiting the amount of results that Yahoo gives you is by telling it exactly where to look. In the options box you can ask it to:

➜ Search the whole of the Yahoo database.

➜ Look for Yahoo categories only

➜ Search only Web sites

➜ Look in Usenet groups

➜ Or only search e-mail addresses

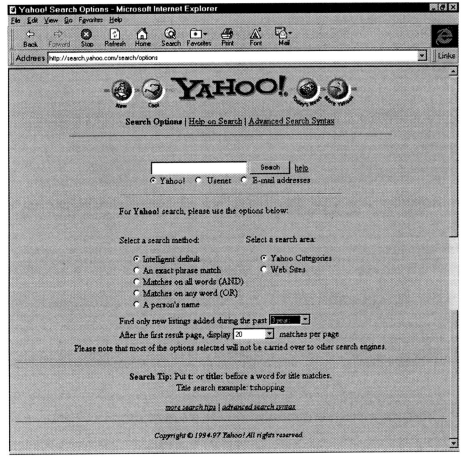

Refining a search with Yahoo

And if you have already done a bit of browsing within Yahoo you will find search boxes which allow you to search the whole of the Yahoo database or only within the category or sub-category you are currently residing.

On the rare occasion that Yahoo retrieves too few sites and/or categories you can try to increase the number of hits by lifting any restrictions that you may have placed on it.

Try not limiting the date so that the engine searches the entire database that it has built up since it was created. Use the "OR" Boolean Operator so that it retrieves the site even if it only uses one of the words that you have typed in.

Also try using wild cards such as the "*" symbol to allow Yahoo a greater selection to choose from.

Other Directories

There are several other directory based search engines that you might like to consider.

Magellan

Not surprisingly all these other directories work in a similar manner to Yahoo. Magellan can be found at: **http:// www.mckinley.com**

The main difference here is that the Magellan indexes give each site a rating from one to four stars. The four star sites are the best (in Magellan's view) and these will be displayed first when you make a search.

Another feature of the Magellan directory is its use of "**green light**" sites which have been passed as safe for children to visit. It is possible to search the database and ask that it returns green light sites only.

Excite

This engine can be found at: **www.excite.com**
and has a look and feel fairly similar to Magellan. Like Yahoo and Magellan you can browse and search but the reviews are fairly limited.

Infoseek

Can be found at: **www.infoseek.com**
is a directory as well as being a robot based search engine.

Nerd World

Is found at: **www.nerdworld.com**
and concentrates on leisure categories and knowledge.

Tip

Magellan contains a feature known as Search Voyeur which allows you to see up to 20 randomly selected search strings that it is currently processing. So if you are just looking around for something to do you can keep an eye on what your fellow surfers are interested in and perhaps get a few ideas.

Active Search Engines

When Web pages are being created at a rate faster than the staff of even Yahoo can keep up with them, there obviously has to be a better way of indexing all the pages on the World Wide Web. The only way that you can possibly hope to do this through automation. So some clever heads got together and created spider programs. These **spiders** roam the Web looking for new URL's and reporting back to base with the details. It may be no exaggeration that one of these programs claims it can index as many as five million new World Wide Web pages each and every hour.

The main difference between the spider based search engines is how they index their information. Obviously since nobody is giving details of the site to the search engine it has to have a way of finding out what the page is all about. This it does by looking at the information on the page itself and sorting it through various programs to decide under which categories the page should be indexed.

False Drops

With the Web robots returning so many pages back to the search engine the databases tend to be on the large side. There is a lot of good information there but there is also a lot of rubbish. So it should come as no surprise, that when you perform the search, you receive back some of the rubbish along with decent information.

But apart from rubbish you will also get decent information which simply is not about the subject that you are looking for. In other words these are pages that include the search string that you put into the engine but use it in a **different context**. These returns are known as "false drops ".

Here is an example. You spent a long night surfing the Web and fancy a coffee in the morning. But you are bored with the same old taste so you would like some ideas for an exotic new brand of coffee for your filter machine. So you trot along to Lycos, enter the word "coffee", and look through the search results. Sure you will find lots of details of different types of coffee and even mail order coffee houses that will send it straight to your door. But you will also find pages on:

- The Coffee Association of Canada
- FAQ's on caffeine abuse
- Software for the point-of-sale in coffee shops
- Lots of pages on the Java programming language
- Sit down coffee shops in Beanhampton, New York
- How to join the Coffee Brewers Federation, and
- A newspage on coffee merchants sealing a new deal!
- The bigger the database the more false drops you will get.

Infoseek

Found at: **www.infoseek.com**

This is one of the largest databases to be found on the Web. It is a combination of directory and spider based search engines and attempts to index everything that it finds. So no level of importance is given to the occurrence of words on a page, or the context in which they appear.

As a result you will get an awful lot of false drops. But you will also retrieve documents that only mention the words you are searching for as a side line. This can be good as well as bad; false drops take a long time to wade through but you will be sure to find something on even the most obscure of subjects.

To get some indication of the size of the databases created by the spider programmes we entered a search for the words "steep skiing" into each of them. Infoseek returned by far the largest number of pages, with a massive 110,418!! Well, I suppose we did require some information on steep skiing and we certainly got it.

AltaVista

Found at: **www.altavista.digital.com**

(note the 'digital', without this you get different site)

This is another of the larger databases to be found on the Web. Just like Infoseek, AltaVista indexes everything it finds on a page. No surprise then that our search for the words "steep skiing" returned 61,585 hits. But on the plus side the more relevant sites did seem to appear at the top of the list. Whatismore, the couple of lines of text put your search into context as it appears on the page so that you can scan through the list of hits fairly quickly.

Like Infoseek you should use AltaVista when you are looking for something fairly obscure and are having problems locating anything on the other search engines.

Lycos

Lycos can be found at: **www.lycos.com**

and differs from Infoseek and AltaVista in that it does not index the full text of a page. Instead it tends to use only the "important" words in a document which it believes to be the title, the headings and around the first 20 lines of the text. It also takes note of hidden tags that Web page creators put in known as "Meta tags".

This technique is used as a simple way of measuring what the page is all about. The logic states that the creator of a Web page will try to get

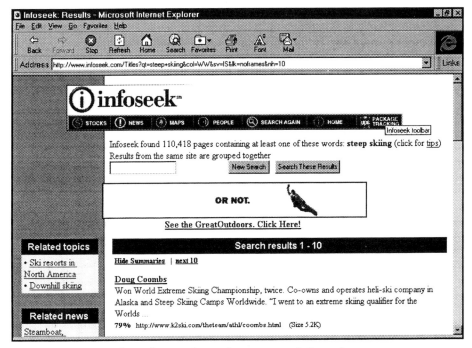

Infoseek search engine at www.infoseek.com

across their main information as early as possible and that the headings will give a good indication as to what the following text is all about.

Our search for "steep skiing" produced a miserly 835 hits which was a fairly good choice and they were all high quality. An excellent result.

Perhaps one of the best parts of Lycos' retrievable system is the fact that it gives you the retrieval score along side the title of the page. This is a ranking out of 100% as to the confidence that Lycos puts on its results. So a score of 100% will indicate that Lycos thinks it is certain it has found information that you are looking for.

A retrieval score of 90% will indicate that it thinks it is highly likely you will want this information but there is also a chance that it is a false drop.

Another neat feature appears right at the top of the retrieved hits. Just in case we hadn't got the information that we were requiring Lycos gave us the option to find more results in these areas:

● Pictures about steep skiing

● Personal home pages about steep skiing

● Books about steep skiing

- Reviews about steep skiing
- and Yellow Pages of steep skiing, whatever that may be. (Perhaps I should give it a try next time and see if there is a company near Harrogate offering steep skiing!)

HotBot

Another huge database to be found at: **www.hotbot.com** which uses a different relevance scoring system to Lycos.

Our search of the steep skiing produced 5,975 results similarly ranked with a percentage relevance score.

WebCrawler

This is supposed to be a slightly smaller database than the rest and can be found at: **www.webcrawler.com**

However it still returned 19,356 hits for steep skiing and is a personal favourite.

Excite

Yet another large database which can be found at: **www.excite.com** which provides some information for the Magellan directory.

Expanding Your Search

Just as with a directory search you can get more or less hits by:
- Using Boolean operators such as AND, OR and NOT.
- Searching for complete phrases
- Using wildcard characters.

Metacrawlers

If you want to take a scatter gun approach to your Web searching pop along to: **www.metacrawler.com**

for a search engine which does not even have its own database. This engine lives off the others and when you enter a search string it consults databases of the leading search engines which have already been mentioned and then generates a retrievable list in its own format.

More Information

As you can see using search engines is more complex than it may appear on the surface. The quality and amount of information that you receive is highly dependent on the search string that you enter into the engine, and the choice of engine in the first place.

If you would like to learn more about search engines and how to get the best out of them then I can recommend "**Find What You Want on the Internet**" by Mark Neely and also published by Net.Works. More details can be seen on page 110.

Tax Self Assessment Made Easy

Stefan Bernstein has distilled the jargon down to a simple easy-to-follow guide **at a price the ordinary taxpayer can afford**.

The book tells you what you have to do and when to do it, warning you of what happens if you don't. Chapters include:
- Self employed and the effects.
- Directors and trustees.
- Record keeping requirements.
- Penalties and surcharges.
- Information for employed people on PAYE.
- What companies need to do.

A valuable glossary and a variety of concise appendices make this book the complete and essential guide with schedules to help you ensure that your tax bill is correct in the first place.

Price: £5.99 - *Ordering information on page 112*

Chapter 6

Shopping in Cyberspace

F OR ANYBODY who is not heavily into shopping the World Wide Web is an absolute boom. And even for those who have problems hanging onto their money and just love to shop-till-they-drop the Web is an absolute wonderland.

Just about everything new which comes along is condemned by old stick-in-the-muds as something which will "never catch on". And, just as before, they have been proved totally wrong. Perhaps it was said by traditional shop owners as much in hope as anything else but here are a number of reasons why shopping on the World Wide Web has caught on and why it is set to be one of the faster growing arenas of human activity this century.

Why?

O kay so you can buy books, compact discs, computer equipment, clothes, airline tickets, cars, underwear, holidays, food, etc., etc., on the World Wide Web, but why should anybody actually do it? Here's why:

Saving time. When you shop on the World Wide Web you are not limited to how far you can walk around the shops in your lunchtime or how long it takes to drive to the nearest town in your car.

Nor do you have to turn up at the shops when it suits them between the hours of 9 till 5, or 4pm at weekends! On the Web your keyboard can do the walking and you can compare the prices between different outlets within seconds.

It is simply far more convenient to sit in front of your computer, when you want, than to traipse all around the shops and still not find what you want.

Selection. The World Wide Web is particularly well suited to products which come in a large number of varieties. For example books and compact discs.

There are almost 100,000 new books published in the UK every year so even if you could find a shop that stocks all of them it would take you forever to find the one that you want. But the Web offers a perfect solution as you do not have to look at the physical book itself.

Instead you can simply enter a search string and have your computer produce a list of books on the topic that you are searching for. Better still, as you will see later in this chapter, you can get reviews on the books from your fellow surfers and compare it to all other available titles with the same information.

It costs less. Going into town to go shopping can be a costly affair. First of all you have the petrol for your car to consider which is a direct cost, but you also have to fork out for lunch and perhaps a coffee just to keep you sane. Then you have got savings on shoe leather to consider not to mention the cost of the tranquillisers that you will need when you get home.

Discounts. Shops on the World Wide Web have far fewer overheads and do not need to employ half as many staff. They do not need expensive floor space on High Streets and they do not need to heat the building to keep you comfortable.

Therefore they can afford to sell the products much cheaper than a standard high street shop. As a result the World Wide Web offers a huge amount of discounts over standard products that you can find in your local town.

What-is-more the immediacy of the Internet enables you to search harder for a better price for the same product amongst the different sets of retailers than it is on the high street. How often have you bought something only to find it cheaper four shops along.

The searchability of the Web combined with the time savings should ensure that you always come up with the best deal.

It's nicer. Unless you are in need of serious help you cannot possibly enjoy going out in the freezing rain on a cold dark night after work (why is it that shops are open from 9 - 5 when most people work the same hours?).

Then who likes pushing through all those noisy crowds, fighting for some personal space inside a shop, and then emerging into the traffic fumes of a congested city. By the time you get home you are normally, dirty, wet, and tired - rather like a drowned rat!

Why Not?

Given all of the above you might be tempted to think why you would ever want to go shopping on the High Street again. But here are a couple of reasons why not to "shop the Web":

Security. Perhaps it is because of the media, but a lot of people have concerns over the security of payments on-line. Without a doubt it is possible to intercept your credit card details when you transmit them from your computer to a server as you place an order. For more information see later in this chapter.

Delivery time. A lot of on-line sites such as the worlds biggest in amazon.com make a big deal about how quick they despatch your goods. Despite having more than 2 million titles to choose from, amazon.com say they will despatch your books within 1-2 days.

On the surface of it this looks like an extremely good service. But what you fail to think about at the time is how long it will take for the goods to reach you. Sure amazon.com may put them in the mail within 2 days but you still have to wait for the postal system to get the goods to your door.

Security

Let's get one thing straight. **The World Wide Web is NOT full of vagabonds out to fleece the whole of mankind from the fruits of their labour.** The whole issue of security on the World Wide Web is largely a media-led concern. As is the way in this country anything the media does not fully understand they like to sensationalise as a way of selling more newspapers and magazines. Just as we have not all died from flesh eating viruses (another media favourite scare story) so those who shop regularly on the World Wide Web have not had their bank accounts cleared out, their personal details altered, or their granny's maiden name changed by forged Deed Poll.

Obviously somewhere along the line somebody has been ripped off on the World Wide Web be-

Hear sound clips before you buy at: www.cdnow.com

cause there is no smoke without fire. But it seems to be a case of an awful lot of smoke from a couple of glowing cinders.

The main bug bear to buying things on the World Wide Web has always been the secure transmittal of data and, in particular **credit card details**. Until recently it has been virtually impossible to guarantee that no one could intercept your credit card details when you are transmitting them from your computer to that of the retailer. The concern is that somebody in a far flung city or town will intercept these details and go around spending your money before they can be detected.

There are two main flaws with the argument that the doom-mongers put forward in this scenario.

First of all it is extremely difficult to intercept information on the World Wide Web. Yes, it is possible, but how many people do you know with the technical expertise to place "packet sniffers" in the gateway to a retailer's host computer?

And secondly, **you stand exactly the same amount of risk by giving your credit card details to a person in a shop, saying them over the telephone or sending them in the regular mail**. This is because the majority of credit card fraud is actually perpetrated by the employees of companies who have legitimate access to your card details - in other words the company that you are sending the details to in the first place.

Just think about it. When you buy something with your credit card in a shop anybody who is standing around could write down the numbers from your card along with the expiry date. They would also be able to see how you sign your signature and it would not be beyond the ability of man to find out your address.

Certainly the person working behind the till will have a permanent record of the credit card number, the expiry date, your signature and your home address (for the guarantee).

Nevertheless it is a concern of people so the 'minds that be' on the World Wide Web are making progress to making it safer to send your credit card details down the line.

Secure Connection

You can be sure that nobody can intercept your credit card details on the World Wide Web if you have established a "secure connection". This connection, between your Browser and the computer you are interacting with, uses a secret, or **scrambled**, communication channel which prevents anybody intercepting the information whilst its en-route.

If you are using Microsoft Internet Explorer you know that you have established a secure connection by looking at the status bar along the bottom of the window. At the right hand side you will see a **lock** appear if you have accessed a secure site. When the lock is visible it is okay to send your information.

With Netscape Navigator you can tell you have established a secure connection by the key icon. A **complete key** indicates that you have got a secure connection, whilst a broken key indicates it is no longer secure.

Certificates

When you go to a site on the Web that makes out that it is a shop, how do you know that it is what it says it is? It may look like an on-line shop but it could quite easily be a site set up by a hacker who has directed your Browser from the true intended site to their computer. You could then be happily sending your credit card details for goods and services which simply do not exist and the hacker walks away with all your details to do their dirty deeds.

It also works in reverse. When you go into that shop, how do the shop owners know you really are

Tip

When you enter a site that says it has a secure server you may not immediately see an unbroken key or a lock on your Browser. This is not an indication that the company is telling lies it is just that secure connections often do not start up until you are on the ordering page.

who you say you are. You could have quite easily stolen somebody's credit card and be using it to shop on-line.

The Internet Bookshop
www.bookshop.co.uk

Get 10% off all books
Do you have a '.ac.uk'
after your name ?
You could win a

COMPAQ

Book of the Week

Aftermath
40% discount
From Star Trek's Lt Cmdr Geordi LaForge, actor-turned-writer LeVar Burton, comes a powerful, disturbing novel of the future. AD 2000-2019: the first African-American president is assassinated...

Title Search

[   ] [GO]

Add Active Channel

New this Week
Have a look at the new Book of the Month for The Business and Management Floor. Money, Madness and Misery

iBS Stop Press
Are you one of millions of Star Wars fans? Want to win selected bestselling Star Wars titles? Go to our new Star Wars feature and take your chance at our competition. Take a look at our Modern Language Departments, featuring the new David Crystal book, The Encyclopedia of English, and the modern language dictionaries no good bookshelf should be without

Utilise the real potential of

The answer being developed for the World Wide Web is known as "**certificates**". This is a form of identification card which is generated by an independent third party. Certificate ca-

Search more than a million titles at:
www.bookshop.co.uk

pabilities are built into most of the latest Browsers including Internet Explorer and Navigator but the system of certificates is still in its infancy.

Before long you will be able to obtain certificates from agencies - perhaps they will be free, or maybe you will have to pay a small fee such as £10 - which will enable you to shop on the Web free of any worries.

On-line Validation

As indicated above, the main risk with credit card details lies with humans who are the intended recipients of the details, but who are also fraudulent. Bearing this in mind, but also in the interest of efficiency, on-line validation systems have been developed. So in the future, when you transmit your credit card details, these will go direct to a bank or third party where they will be validated by a computer.

Authorisation codes will then be transmitted to the retailer in order to allow them to collect your money. **At no time will a human come in contact with your card details.** This on-line validation, combined with the use of certificates, will make shopping on the World Wide Web far more secure, and even safer than shopping on the High Street.

Alternatives

If, after everything that has been said, you still have reservations about sending your credit card details over the World Wide Web then there are some very simple alternatives. Most shops will provide you with a phone number so that you can call through with your credit card details or there will also be a fax number where you can fax through your order.

To save you time writing everything out why not simply print out the order form by hitting the print button on your Browser and then completing it and faxing it through to the company? You could also use the same method for sending an order through the traditional mail system.

One final possibility is for you to send your order by way of two separate e-mails. In the first e-mail you send your credit card number and part of your order and in the second e-mail you send the expiry date for your credit card and your address details. It would be extremely difficult for anybody to intercept both of these e-mails and match them up, but the person receiving them will find it much easier. The difficulty for the fraudulent hacker here is that packet sniffers are designed to search out text strings which may look like credit card details. Neither of your e-mails will have this appearance so they will have a far lower chance of being intercepted.

Selection of Shops

If you have not really already looked here are a selection of shops that you will find on the World Wide Web with a few of the features that you will find in many other stores.

The Internet Book Shop

This is Europe's answer to *amazon.com.* At its heart is a database of all the books ever published in the United Kingdom and the United States of America.

Indeed, if a book has been published through the normal trade system in the English language the Internet Book Shop should be able to get hold of a copy for you or at least tell you it is out of print. Because they do not have all the overheads of a High Street shop you will find lots of discounts of up to 50%.

Two of the best features of the book shop is its ability to search for the books that you want and the reviews offered by your fellow surfers.

Unlike a normal book shop where you are reliant on the shop assistant and their willingness to look up information for you, you can use the **search facility** to look for titles of books with key words, find all books produced by a certain author, look for the range of titles from a particular publisher, and search by international standard book number.

Once you have retrieved a list of books that you may be interested in you can have a look at reviews written by fellow surfers and/or those published in the media.

For a lot of titles you can also retrieve an image of the front cover and find all the bibliographic details for the title.

The Internet Bookshop can be found at: **www.bookshop.co.uk**

Compact Discs

Another area mentioned above where the sheer number of volumes available is too large for a human to be able to search through.

CD Now (**www.cdnow.com**) is a virtual compact disc shop which gives you the chance to search through not only albums but also tracks to find the one that you want.

The big benefit of this shop is that you are able to **listen to tracks** from certain albums while you are looking through the shop. Of course you will need certain plug-in's for your Browser but more of that in the next chapter.

Lands End

This is the on-line version of the mail order catalogue that you probably receive through your letter box a couple of times every year. If you have already bought from the traditional Lands End catalogue then you will be familiar with ordering an item that you cannot touch and feel. Therefore you have absolutely no problems ordering from their World Wide Web version of the catalogue.

The benefit of this site is the **rate of information update**. For example, the overstock items are put onto the site every week or so. With the speed that fashion changes people's taste you can find some excellent bargains in these overstocks with clothes being discounted at up to 50% off their normal catalogue price.

It would obviously be far too costly for Lands End to hand out up dates to their traditional catalogue for items that they are going to discount every week. But their costs of doing so on the World Wide Web are so small that this can be a profitable way to remainder lines on which they have over bought.

The World of Gambling

Where the Internet Bookshop can offer you a huge selection to choose from, CD Now can allow you to listen to the tracks before you buy and

Lands End can offer you weekly discount lines on their overstocks, *The World of Gambling* does not offer a particularly huge range, it does not give free samples and it does not discount many lines.

However this is an excellent example of a **niche shopping** site on the World Wide Web. It probably would not be cost effective to open a shop on the High Street specialising in gambling products. That is because no population centre would be large enough to support such a shop.

But with everybody in the country a potential customer for a World Wide Web shop, the target audience becomes large enough to support such a shop.

From the consumer's point of view it is also a benefit. This is because you are highly unlikely to find any book shop stocking gambling titles. There simply isn't enough demand to do so. Nor would you find your local computer shop with a huge array of gambling software for the same reason. And if you wanted to buy a pair of original casino dice where would you start to look?

This on-line store which can be found at :

www.gamble.co.uk

brings together gambling books on everything from blackjack to lotteries and roulette to spread betting, software, accessories, systems and even gambling games.

Buying On-line

The biggest obstacle to buying something on-line is probably your own concerns over security. Assuming these can be fulfilled by secure connections or the use of certificates, then buying something is simplicity itself.

In the majority of shops you can look through their catalogues and departments to find products that you are interested in. Once you have spotted an item write down its reference number or remember what it is called and then go to the page which is the order form. This may come in one of two forms:

● An on-line form where you fill in boxes and then hit a submit button. In this case your information is then transmitted by way of a CGI script to the shop's computer.

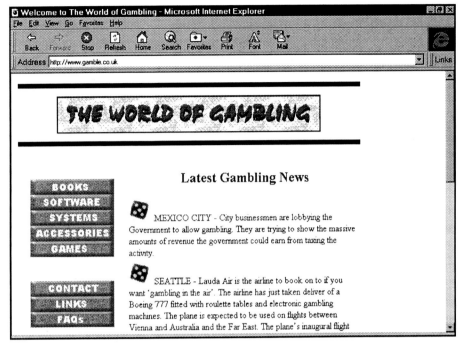

Niche marketing on the Web at its best: www.gamble.co.uk

● A traditional form which you download onto your computer and then send back to the shop either as an e-mail, a fax or through the traditional mail .

Larger shops sometimes offer you the use of an on-line shopping basket. This is just like using a shopping trolley in a supermarket. When you see a product that you like then you click on a button which adds it to your virtual basket. When you reach the end of your Browsing session you then take your basket to the order page where the total bill is added up and your credit card details are requested.

Once you have handed over your details, by whatever method, the transaction is completed and you can look forward to the receipt of your goods. If you sent your order electronically a lot of shops will send you an electronic confirmation of your order. And if there should be a problem with your order such as a supplier not sending them to the shop in time then you will receive details in your e-mail.

Chapter 7

Sound, Motion, & VRML

IT WILL BE pretty obvious from Chapter 3 that your Browser is a clever piece of software. Not only will it display pictures and text but it will also allow you to navigate your way around the World Wide Web. But as every upgrade goes by they get more and more like little operating systems.

A lot of the development of Browsers is being driven by the World Wide Web itself. The primary function of the Web may well still be the provision of information but running a close second must be entertainment. Indeed, surveys in America where people have been monitored to see when they surf the World Wide Web, has indicated that the time they use to go on-line is substituted time that they ordinarily would have spent in front of the television set.

To meet this demand for entertainment, and to meet marketing ideals where commercial sites are concerned, Browsers are becoming equipped with tools to perform a whole array of new functions.

One of the simplest things a Web site developer can do to his site to improve it is to add moving image files. As opposed to movies themselves these are quite simply images that they have created which when played altogether give the appearance of movement. An example of this can be seen on a site that has been mentioned many times before:

www.gamble.co.uk/books.htm

Here you can see two animated gifs; a rotating smiley face indicating the "book of the month" and a red flash which appears to travel along the black rule underneath *The World of Gambling* banner.

To create the rotating smiley the site builder will have drawn first the smiling face square on and then would have created the second image with the face rotated a small number of degrees. The next image would have shown it rotated a few more degrees and then the next one more degrees still. When all these "images" (actually they are compressed into one image) are downloaded as shown one after another they give the appearance of movement rather like those flick through books that you may have made as a child.

But in this modern day of rapidly accelerating Web technology, moving gifs are indeed child's play.

Music on the Web

For you to be able to hear a sound that is associated with a Web page your Browser needs to download a file that contains the information for your computer to use. Once received your computer is able to decipher the information with the help of a program (see below) and play it back to you if you have a sound card and speakers attached to your computer.

To be able to deal with a sound file your Browser will need some help unless it has already been pre-loaded with the method of dealing with sound files. It will either need a helper application which is a program stored on your computer that starts automatically when the sound file is received. Or it could use a plug in (discussed in chapter 3) which slots into your Browser and runs as part of the Browser program. Finally it could use an ActiveX control which works like a plug-in but is effectively using Windows 95 to seamlessly link program files together.

You don't have to worry too much, if at all, about the helper applications, plug ins, and ActiveX controls that your Browsers will need since the designers of the Browsers have done virtually everything for you.

If your requirements are not already loaded into the Browser that you receive from your Internet Access Provider and the Browser comes across a music file then you will be automatically prompted by the Browser to download the application.

All you have to do is click "OK" on the little window that has prompted you and the application will be downloaded onto your computer, linked to the Browser and will be fully functional within a couple of minutes. From this point onwards you will be able to use it to interpret the files and listen to the sounds it is designed to play.

You will notice the qualification in the last sentence of the last paragraph. The application will play the files "that it is designed to play". This is because there is no single agreed file format for transmitting sounds across the WWW. Just as in the early days of video recording you could have opted for BETA format or VHS so the options on sound files have yet to be consolidated. There are four main types of sound file that you may come across on the Web:

Windows sound. These files have a ***.wav** extension and a standards window sound - meaning they will be the most common that you will see on the Web. They play back very good quality sound (near CD quality if you have a good sound card and speakers). But the down side is that these files are often very big and take a long time to download.

MPEG Stereo. These files have a ***.mp2** extension and offer quality stereo sound along with a good compression ratio, so the files are not quite so big.

Mixed Sound. These sound files have a ***.au** extension and exhibit an excellent compression ratio making them fairly small. Unfortunately the sound quality suffers and the sound is usually only mono.

Apple Sound. These files may have one of three extensions ***.aifc**, ***.aiff**, or ***.aif.** They only come as mono.

Playing a Sound

Most of the sounds that you come across on World Wide Web pages need to be fully downloaded onto your computer before you can play them back through your speakers. The exception is "streaming sound" which we will discuss in a moment.

To play a sound that you have found on a page simply click or double click on the link. Your Browser will then start up an audio player and once the file has finished downloading the player will start to function automatically.

If you are using Navigator or Internet Explorer you can play the sound again by clicking on the "play again" button, or you can listen to part of the sound by moving the slider along the scale to the part of the file that you would like to hear.

Streaming Sound

There is a fairly well developed format for streaming sound known as **RealAudio**. The difference with these files is that they start playing as

soon as your computer starts to receive them. This is in contrast to all the other sound formats where your computer must receive the full file before you can play it back. As it has been indicated that sound files are often quite large, this is a real benefit.

The down side is that the quality is not very good and it is rather like listening to an old medium wave signal in bad weather.

However, it is used primarily for voice recordings as a way of giving you commentary as you move around the Web site.

Moving Pictures

Video clips are becoming avail-able on an ever increasing number of sites. You can catch a glimpse of Michael Jordan hanging a shot, and see your favourite band perform a chord or two. But don't expect to see too much action, and be prepared to get your magnifying glass out. For video clips on the Web are neither large in size nor in length.

The reason behind both of these restrictions is the size of the files that are needed. Even for playing a little video clip in the very corner of your screen for less than 60 seconds you will find that the file re-quired (which is as compressed as the makers can get it) will be around about a megabyte in size.

Even with a fast modem and at a quiet time of the day this will still take quite a few minutes to download. Since streaming video still has not been developed this is lost time. And you cannot even go around other pages on the Web whilst you are downloading the file because to do so would slow the file transfer rate even further.

As with sound the format for video movies has not been agreed. The three main formats that you will come across are:

MPEG. This is short for Motion Picture Experts Group and is the oldest format. The compression rate is high so the download times are low, but the quality of the clips are not very good.

QuickTime Movies. This is Apple's standard and is possibly the best of the bunch. You get a good quality video and accompanying mono or stereo sound. Both Navigator and Internet Explorer can play QuickTime Movies despite it being an Apple standard.

Video for Windows. Competition for Apple's movie standard comes in the form of ***.avi** files which is Windows' preferred movie format. The files are the biggest on offer but they also bring with it improved quality and often accompanying stereo sound.

Playing a Movie

The way in which you see a movie in your Browser will depend on the player that you are using. Most of them, though, have similar features and resemble standard VCR's. You get a play button, a pause button, and fast forward and fast back, but the extras that you get over the top of the VCR control is a sliding scale which will allow you to move continuously to any part of the movie so you can watch it over again.

Virtual Reality

The next step for your Browser is for it to be able to display images in three dimensions. This is where VRML controls come in. It is short for Virtual Reality Modelling Language and gives Web Masters the ability to make sites that show a three dimensional perspective. Just as when you access music and video, the plug-in's for these start automatically.

The main use of VRML sites is currently for playing games. You move around a landscape performing tasks and interacting with other characters in the game.

Moving around is fairly complicated but by default it assumes that you are "walking" and that you are "on the ground". To go forward you drag your mouse up, and to go back you drag your mouse down.

Drag to the right to turn right, and drag to the left to go left. Each time you move you will see the three dimensional world displayed in your Browser change as if you were a real person moving around a virtual landscape.

Java

Since your Browser can play sounds, movie clips and even move you around a three dimensional landscape the next step is obviously to get it to run a miniature program. And this is where Sun Microsystems have developed a programming language known as "**Java**".

Both Navigator and Internet Explorer are Java-capable Browsers and can play Java programs downloaded from Web pages.

These miniature paragraphs are known as "**applets**" and give a certain functionality to your Browser. What the little Java applet does is only limited by the Web site Developer's imagination but it could be anything from a working clock to a functional spread sheet. The oddest applet I have seen is a miniature ouji board where you can move the glass over the table by placing your mouse over the top of it. The Java applet then spells out a word or phrase which I needed to enter a competition.

There are **security implications** that come along with Java since loading a program onto your computer automatically could cause problems. It is not beyond the realms of possibility for somebody to make a bad applet that could harm your hard drive. This, however, should not concern you too much since Java does not have any commands that would allow access to your file systems.

ActiveX Controls

These controls work with your Browser as a sort of miniature container for any programs. This allows Web Masters to create sites in a language that they prefer such as Java, visual basic, or C++.

This makes ActiveX more versatile than Java but it also makes it **more dangerous**. This is because ActiveX gives full access to your computer's file system.

So a rogue program could quite easily wipe your hard disk clean. For this reason a little warning box will appear in your Browser before any ActiveX control is downloaded.

This will ask you if you want to download your control and should also display the "program certificate". The certificate is a form of validation which comes from an independent third party and vouches that the program is trustworthy.

Myth: The WWW is all American.

Truth: Take a trip to www.yahoo.co.uk and write down all the British URLs you find. After a few days scribbling you should change your mind!

Downloading from the WWW

Chapter 8

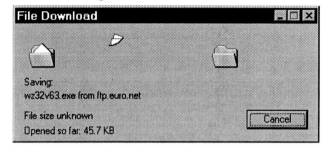

PLAYING MUSIC, watching videos and watching three-dimensional worlds with your Browser may be good entertainment but the World Wide Web is far more useful than that. All over the Web you will find sites where you can easily download files and programs for running on your computer which have nothing to do with the Browser.

Software such as utilities, games, virus checkers, patches for Windows 95, screensavers, spreadsheets, typing tutors, and much, much, more. Indeed, if it is possible to do something with your computer then you will find a program somewhere along the World Wide Web that you can download direct.

These programs on the Web come in three forms:

Public Domain Programmes. These can be copied freely and distributed without hindrance. They can even be modified and resold without the author's permission.

Freeware. This is software made available free of charge by the author but are still under copyright, and certain conditions may apply.

Shareware. This, again, is copyrighted software and you are free to evaluate it on your computer free of charge. But once the evaluation period is up, usually around a month, and you found the software to be useful then you should pay a registration fee to the author for continued use of the program.

There are probably around about half a million public domain, freeware and shareware programmes available on the World Wide Web if you search hard enough, and the good news, this time around, is that there is an accepted format of the compression of the files that you come across. These files are known as **"zip files"** (not to be confused with Iomega's Zip Drive).

These files all appear with an extension of ***.zip** or with an extension ***.exe** once you have downloaded them. There are, of course, other forms of file available on the World Wide Web most notably the *.sit files cre-

Top downloads from shareware.com

ated for Macintosh's and *.z, *.gz and *.tar files for UNIX computers. However these are few and far between and around 95% will be zip files.

The even better news is that all of these files (including the Macintosh and UNIX files) can be decompressed using a single program. This program is itself shareware and is known as **WinZip** and is produced by *Nico Mac Computing.*

Without a shadow of a doubt this utility is a **"must have"**. Without it you will not be able to decompress files that you downloaded from the World Wide Web and so you won't be able to use the programs. Besides, you will find it an extremely useful utility outside of your World Wide Web life for compressing and archiving files on your own hard disk.

Compression

Program files are often very large in terms of bytes or Megabytes. So putting them on the Web and downloading them would not be very practicable.

This is because even with a fast modem it would take a long time to download them and tie up your phone lines for long periods. However if these files are compressed into a "zip file" they take up much less space and download far quicker.

Obviously the software which performs such compression has to be fairly clever so that he can make the file smaller but, when asked, will restore it to its exact original format (computer programs are extremely pedantic and even a slight change in the code will cause the whole thing to fail).

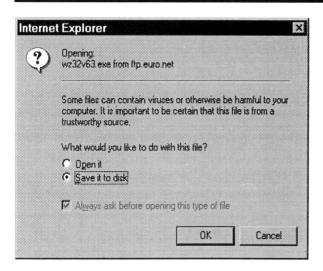

Before downloading a file, you'll be asked if you want to save it to your hard disk or open it immediately.

The way that WinZip and other compression programs work is by looking at the programs and spotting long, repeated information-lines in the programming code. Each of these regularly repeated sequences can then be replaced with an abbreviation. Then, when decompression is required, the original long sequence is substituted for the abbreviation.

WinZip is extremely efficient in this procedure and you will be amazed at how small it can make even the largest of files. And on top of this it allows you to "**archive**" files into the same zip file. So one compressed file can contain many original files such as the program, a readme file, special drivers, and a registration form. Indeed, if you find yourself downloading sophisticated programs - and it is possible to even download program suites such as Office 97 - the zip file may contain hundreds of archive files.

Other popular Internet file formats supported by WinZip include:

- ✔ TAR
- ✔ gzip
- ✔ UUencode
- ✔ XXencode

- ✔ BinHex
- ✔ MINE
- ✔ UnixCompress
- ✔ *.arj, *.lzh and *.arc (via external programs).

Downloading

In this section you will kill two birds with one stone because you will see how you can use your Browser to download files from the World Wide Web, and the example file downloaded will be the latest version of WinZip!

Fire up your Browser and connect to the World Wide Web. Then, in the address box, type the following:-

shareware.com

and hit return.

This will take you to an excellent shareware site run by C|NET. Here you will find the largest number of programs available on the World Wide Web and you will probably never need to look any further.

On the home page you will see that you are able to search its database of hundreds of thousands of

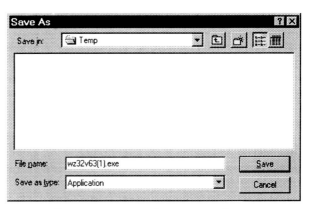

Save compressed programs into a temporary directory.

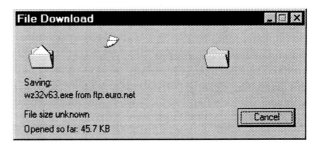

If the download is taking too long, cancel the transfer and try another site.

programs or you can Browse through the files using the categories listed. You will also see three "special" categories for the **most popular files** downloaded from the site, the newest titles added to the site, and the top picks by the shareware.com team.

Probably the easiest way to get your WinZip utility is to click on "most popular" in the categories. WinZip is such an important utility that it almost always features in the most popular list.

You will then be presented with a screen which looks similar to the one shown on page 46. When this screen shot was taken you will see that the latest version of WinZip is the most popular of the most popular files. This particular service release (an upgrade to take care of a small bug) has only been out for four weeks and has spent three of those in the number one slot. On the week in question no less than 14,341 Web surfers have downloaded the file to their computer.

On the right of the statistics you will see the file name which is wz32v63.exe in this example. However you may need to look down the list of files and read the descriptions to find the latest version by the time you come to this site.

Once you have located the file click on the file name which will be a hyperlink to the download screen.

Here you will be presented with a list of sites (computers) from where you can download the WinZip file. These are listed alphabetically and include a reliability guide to give you some indication of how easy it is to connect to the site without any problems.

The best strategy here is to try and pick a site not necessarily closest to you but one which will be quiet when you want to download the file. If you are trying to download the file in the morning then perhaps the best sites to go to are in the USA when most people will be asleep whereas if you are in the afternoon and the Americans are awake then you are better downloading from somewhere like Australia.

Click on the file name at a site that you think is suitable. Your Browser will then open a window informing you of the file you are about to download and from which site.

There will probably be a warning that files downloaded from the World Wide Web could contain viruses. The shareware.com site will fall into the **trustworthy** source category but if you are still wary then you can check the file for potential viruses once you have downloaded it.

You will also be asked if you would like to save the file to disk or to open it immediately. This is down to personal preference but saving it to disk is usually the least confusing option to take. It is also the cheapest in terms of connection time.

Once you click on the "OK" button you will be prompted as to which folder you wish to put the file into. Select a **temporary directory** somewhere on your hard disk such as C:\temp or C:\windows\temp.

Then click on "save". Your Browser will then open yet another window indicating that the file is beginning to download and showing you how many bytes of information have been transferred.

If you made a note of the **file size** from the download page at shareware.com you will be able to get an idea of how quick the downloading will be. If you follow the advice of connecting to a computer where the local population will be asleep you should not have any problems. But if the file transfer seems to be taking too long it could be a good strategy to hit the cancel button and then connect to a different site.

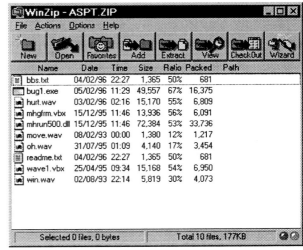

One zipped file can contain hundreds of compressed individual files

Installing WinZip

Close your Browser and disconnect from the World Wide Web. Then go to the directory to which you have downloaded the compressed WinZip file. You will notice that this file has the ***.exe** extension and not the *.zip extension. This is just as well, as without WinZip you would not be able to read the zip file! The *.exe extension indicates that the file is a **self extracting archive**. This means it will probably be bigger than a zipped file but it contains within it the software needed to extract itself onto your computer.

Either double click on the file or run it from the "Start" icon of Windows 95. Then follow the instructions that will appear on the screen.

During the set up you will be informed that WinZip is itself a shareware program and that you will be allowed to evaluate it for 30 days. After that you should **register** a copy of the program with *Nico Mac*, and the best way of doing this is to send your credit card details. Once registered you will be sent a registration number that you enter into the program and which removes the "reminder" screen from the WinZip startup sequence.

At the end of the setup WinZip will be installed on your computer and will have integrated itself with your Windows desk top.

Try using My Computer or Windows Explorer to open a folder. Now click on any file using the right mouse button. You will see a new option has appeared in the top area of the window which allows you now to add the highlighted file to a zip file directly.

Using WinZip to compress and decompress files on your computer is another story, instead this publication will only deal with it in connection with your Browser.

If you are using Microsoft Internet Explorer you will not need to do anything more. WinZip automatically configures windows so that *.zip files are associated with the program. This means that WinZip will be started up when you double click on *.zip files or when your Browser makes such a request.

Netscape Navigator is a bit different since it is not fully integrated into the desk top. Instead click on the **Options** button of the Browser followed by **General Preferences**. Within Preferences select the "**helpers**" tab and look down the "**file type**" list. Choose **application/x-zip-compressed** and in the "action area" click on the **launch application** radio button. Then use the Browse button to locate your WinZip executable file which you will normally find in

c:\programfiles\winzip folder.

Then finish the sequence by clicking on "open" and "OK".

Congratulations you can now use the "**open it**" option when downloading a file from the World Wide Web and/or can open zip files when you have finished your surfing section.

Understand Shares in a Day

Understand Shares in a Day is an indispensable title which shows how the share market really works. Inexperienced investors will learn:

❑ About different types of shares
❑ Why share prices fluctuate
❑ How to read the financial pages
❑ How shares are bought and sold
❑ How risk can be spread with investment and unit trusts
❑ How to build a portfolio of shares
❑ The risks and rewards associated with Penny Shares

Once this basic groundwork has been covered, the book explores more complex ideas which will appeal to both beginners and more experienced investors alike, including:

● How to value shares
● How technical analysis is used to predict share movements
● How equity options are used by professional investors to 'gear' profits and hedge against falling share prices.

Only £6.95. Please order from page 112, bookshops or **http:// www.net-works.co.uk/ Fbooks.htm**

Chapter 9

Viruses and the Web

Successfully downloading files from the World Wide Web and installing them on your computer is one thing, but how do you know it is safe to do so? It could be that you have just unknowingly downloaded a file that contains a virus. Although this is highly unlikely the consequences are just too horrendous to take the risk.

A virus is a software **program** that attaches itself in secret to an existing program adding some extra instructions. These unwanted instruction then set about having their bit of "fun" by messing with your system.

At their worst they can do some pretty nasty things such as format your entire hard disk, destroying all the data and programs you have so lovingly assembled.

And at best they will simply sit on your system for a long time and sporadically throw up humorous or strange messages when you are least expecting them. The majority, however, fit into the middle ground and attach certain types of program or scramble sections of your data.

In addition to virus codes attaching themselves to programs you may be unlucky enough to come across a "**trojan horse**". These are nasty little characters which mascarade as useful programs but, when run, will do untold damage to your computer.

Signs of a Cold

You can get some indications that your computer may be infected with a virus when:

✗   Your computer slows down inexplicably.

✗   Strange characters appear when you type anything.

✗   Random error messages appear unrelated to what you are doing.

✗   And files are not where you would expect them to be.

Scanning for a Virus

Fortunately there are many anti-virus programs readily available on the market. You can even download some pretty useful anti-virus programs from the shareware site discussed in the last chapter.

These programs check out all programs and/or files on your hard disk for signs of a virus. If they detect any you are alerted and given several solutions to the problem. The most common give you the option to erase the infected file completely, for it to fix the problem, or for it to be removed to a floppy disk.

The problem with these programs is that they need a database of existing viruses to function properly. If you have been unlucky enough to download a file with the latest virus your anti-virus program may not know what it is, so it could reside on your system totally undetected by the anti-virus program and leave you unknowingly spreading the virus to everyone you share information with. The top anti-virus programs, however, partially get around this problem by allowing you to **download the latest virus patterns from their Web sites**. This then up dates your anti-virus database with the imprints of all the latest nasties which have been discovered.

Other forms of anti-virus program run on your computer and continuously monitor for any spurious activity. If they detect anything strange going on such as files being deleted or activities in parts of the computer that would not be expected, you are alerted.

A program which can be recommended, and which will both scan your system for existing viruses and monitor activity around your system, is PC-cillin 95.

Don't Panic!

It is not worth worrying unduly about catching a virus from the World Wide Web. The first thing to realise is that only **executable files** can carry a virus.

This means that **graphic files** are completely safe to download because they are data files. Similarly **text files** cannot carry a virus. Nor can **e-mail** (but attached executables can). That should account for 98% of the stuff you will receive from the World Wide Web.

One set of viruses that appear, on the surface of it, to be an exception to the rule infects Microsoft Word document files and Microsoft Excel spread sheets. But these viruses are actually macro's.

Chapter 10

Bad Stuff and Safeguards

IT IS MORE than likely that you will have read or heard about the amount of bad stuff that is available on the World Wide Web. News-papers and documentaries claim that the Web is crawling with pornographic sites and paedophiles at every corner. Nobody, they say, is safe - least of all the children.

There have been reports of school children being abducted after making appointments to meet somebody they have met via the Web. And other reports of students making bombs at home using instructions they have gained from highly descriptive Web sites.

As a result, debate has raged over the validity of allowing dangerous material onto the Web. Should Internet Service Providers prevent such sites going onto the Web? or should the authorities take a controlling hand? and then what about the freedom of speech? The latter being a particularly strong argument over the pond where freedom of information is a cornerstone of the American Constitution. The World Wide Web is an information resource, they argue, and on-line censorship would be akin to book burning by an out of control dictator.

However it would be a fallacy to deny that there is undesirable material out there on the World Wide Web.

How Many?

Don't ever forget that the media like to sensationalise stories in order to keep you watching and make a name for a producer, or to sell more newspapers off the back of the story. But even bearing that in mind, how many Web sites, in terms of a percentage, do you think are dedicated to sex? And what about the more dangerous news groups. What percentage of those are devoted to sex?

What did you guess? Chances are that you would have gone for something like 10-20% or if you are a pessimist 20-30%. But you may be surprised to learn that less than 1% of news groups are devoted to sex and less than 0.5% of World Wide Web pages are deemed pornographic. Now, by way of a learning exercise, pop down to your local newsagents or garage and calculate the number of pornographic magazines on display as a percentage of the total number!

So it follows that **you are highly unlikely to accidentally stumble across undesirable material on the World Wide Web and this applies regardless of age.**

But perhaps the main problem is something which few experts will admit to. Today's generation are the most advance in terms of computer technology that there have ever been. And they are an inquisitive bunch. No matter how well you hide material that you do not want them to see, they will find it. The deeper you put it the deeper they will dig.

There is also an argument to say that children exposed to the World Wide Web will gain first hand information in areas which adults may consider to be objectionable such as sex, drugs and gambling. This could help them mature faster and to learn for themselves instead of putting up barriers to the morals being pushed at them by over-protective adults. After all, for every Web site which advocates the taking of drugs you will find perhaps 50 which tell you how bad it is.

Stopping the Rot

Even so if you are still concerned about the material that is available on the World Wide Web there are a whole range of software products joining the market which can be used to limit access to such information.

They all work in a similar manner by monitoring the activity of all Internet related programs (not just World Wide Web Browsers) for certain key words and phrases. They function at bit-stream level which means that they monitor the data coming in and out of your computer (via the modem) instead of in the program itself.

This means that children can use any program that they wish, such as a Browser they may have brought home from school, and they still won't be able to bypass the controls.

Netnanny and Cyberpatrol offer ways of protecting children from bad stuff on the Web

At the core is a list of addresses which may contain material that you wish to prohibit. These addresses are categorised into subjects such as:

✔ nudity

✔ drugs

✔ racism

✔ extremist organisations

✔ gambling

✔ cults.

You are then able to limit access to all of these sites or manually override controls for the sites that you may think of as acceptable. Since new sites are coming on-line all the time these databases need to be kept up-to-date and you can usually obtain new files direct from the Web.

Perhaps the most useful function of these programs is to control the information that can be uploaded on to the Web in the first place. These prevent kids from providing personal information about themselves which could be of use to perverts and about your household which could be of use to thieves.

Some programs also allow you to **limit the amount of time** that your children may spend surfing the World Wide Web. First of all they allow you to set the hours that may be spent browsing the Web to a certain number per day or per week, and they will only allow access at a **certain time of the day** so you can stop them sneaking down stairs at the dead of night for a sly surf!

The Future

Faced with the threat of govern-ment intervention and legal restrictions many organisations are taking it onto their own back to do something about objectionable material.

On-line organisations such as CompuServe and AOL have created **kids only services** which only contain material of educational or enter-tainment value. Other sites clearly label what is considered to be children friendly material. This includes search engines such as Magellan, dis-cussed earlier, which mark such sites with a "green light".

Access providers and software companies are also working together in an effort to develop software programming standards that will allow Web Browsers to detect when they are connecting to an adult material site. This will then give you a Browser level control on what can be viewed and what blocked out.

The major hope here is known as PICS (Platform for Internet Con-tents Selection). This is a self regulatory system of rating pages on the Web according to the material that they contain.

For more information on access restriction programs take a look at:
www.netnanny.com
www.cyberpatrol.com, or
www.surfwatch.com

Chapter 11

Building Your Own Page

SOONER OR LATER you are not going to be satisfied with simply surfing the World Wide Web. You are going to want to make your own contribution and publish your own home page. For some people it will come as a surprise that anyone can put a page on the World Wide Web, without having to be a company or well known organisation. But the truth is that anybody with access to the World Wide Web can publish their own site.

There are pluses and minuses to this. On the plus side it means that everybody can have their say and anybody who is interested wherever they are in the world can listen. On the down side it means that an awful lot of complete rubbish is published on the Web making the decent stuff harder to find and slowing down the overall performance of the Internet.

To successfully publish your own page on the Web you need:

Something to say; the easy bit.

The page itself written in HTML, and

Somewhere to put your new page.

Saying Something

You really can put anything that you really like onto the World Wide Web. From a picture of you and your dog and a description of what you like to have for breakfast right through to an in-depth thesis on the space-time continuum and unification theory.

But apart from complete vanity you can use it to help look for a job by publishing your CV, assist in the publicity for a cause you believe deeply in, provide valuable information free of charge to fellow surfers, or to sell something. In fact it is your imagination that provides the limiting factor.

The only thing that you should look out for are pushing back the boundaries of decency.

Even if your morals don't prevent you publishing material that may upset others, your ISP (or whoever you use to store your page) may see it differently. As discussed in the previous chapter the Web is rapidly moving towards the self regulation system and you could soon find yourself excluded.

You also need to make sure that you are not breaking any laws; not only of this land but also in other countries around the world - remember the World Wide Web truly is a global network.

What is more you may find some restrictions placed on you by your Web provider. For example most ISP will not allow you to use free space for commercial activity.

Creating Your Page

This is where it starts to get a little more difficult - but not as hard as you think. Any page that goes onto the World Wide Web needs to be written in **HTML** an acronym for a Hypertext Mark-Up Language. These are essentially ASCII text with codes embedded in them for formatting things like text styles, paragraphs, tables and hyperlinks.

There are almost as many Web page editing programs as there are browsers. Some of these can be best described as a hindrance as opposed to an aid, but to others they are absolutely outstanding.

Two of the best are *HotMetal Pro* from SoftQuad and Adobe's *PageMill*. These programs give you the options of creating your page in raw HTML code, just viewing it in "tags" and WYSIWYG (what you see is what you get).

Using these packages it is almost possible to create a page simply by dragging and dropping elements onto the page and typing in the body text yourself. However, an **understanding** of how HTML works will make the job so much easier and speed the whole process up no end.

Understanding HTML is not hard at all, certainly when compared to normal computer programming. But it is extremely boring and repetitious. It essentially comes down to writing the page that you wish to publish using normal plain text then adding some tags which format the text you have already written, inserting a code of instructions for any images you wish to use, and embedding those all-important hyperlinks to further World Wide Web pages. It would take a complete book in itself to give you all the tricks of the trade concerning HTML. Net.Works publish

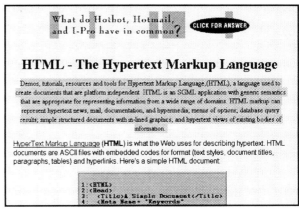

More about HTML at
www.stars.com/Authoring/HTML/

such a book in **Create Your Own Web Site** by Mark Neely - see page 112 for more details. But you can find a decent on-line guide at the following address: **www.stars.com/Authoring/HTML/**

Getting Started

The quickest way to get a page off the ground is to turn to your trusted word processing package. Any will do, including the Windows 95 Notepad. Now type in any line of text that you like, but for this example we will use the string "*This is my first web page*". Now save this page onto your hard disk as **mypage.htm**.

Having done that, fire up your Web Browser, but instead of connecting to the www go to the file command and select "open" then use the "browse" button to locate the file you have just created. Click "OK" and you should find that your Browser displays the text that you have just typed in. Congratulations this is your first page of HTML and it could go up on to the World Wide Web already if you should so wish!

Tags

Whilst there remains the option of simply putting up lines of text like you have already made it really would not be all that enticing, easy-to-read and you would not get many return visitors.

To start adding a bit more visual impact you will need to use "**tags**". These tags tell Browsers how to display the text that you typed into your page. They usually come in pairs; One at the beginning of the text and one at the end. And every time you want to change the look of a piece of text you need to end the tag style that you are using and start a new one.

Go back to your word processing package and open your file "mypage.htm". Now place your cursor in front of the word "first", and type:

<B>

then move the cursor to the end of the word "first" and type:

</B>

and save the page again.

Returning to your Browser which should still be displaying your line of text, take your mouse up and click on the **refresh** button. And you should find that the word "first" is now displayed in bold.

Go back, again, to your word processing package and this time place your cursor before the word "page" and type:

<I>

and move it to the end of the line and type:

</I>

and again save the document.

Now using your Web Browser click on "refresh" again and you will find that the word "page" has turned to italics.

This time stay in your Browser and go up to the "view" command. Click on it and go down to the "source" command. You should find that the Windows editor Notepad automatically opens in a new Window

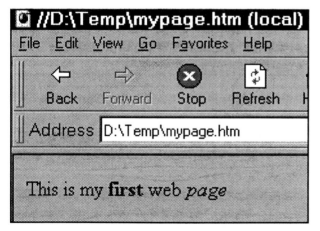

and displays your new page in HTML format.

Use your cursor to delete the italic tags that you have just inserted. Then close the Notepad Editor saving your changes. Press the "refresh" button again and you will see that the italics have disappeared.

You should be getting the idea by now. The tags are used to bracket the piece of text that you wish to format and always (well, nearly) come in pairs.

Headings

Return to the "view source" command from your Browser and display your HTML code again. Place the cursor to the beginning of the text and enter two carriage returns. Now go to the top of the page and type "This is the heading". Return your cursor to the beginning and enter the tag:

<H1>

then to the end of the heading text that you have just typed and insert:

</H1>

and save the file again. This time when you press the "refresh" button you will see that "This is a heading" is now displayed in large text.

Repeat the exercise but this time instead of inserting "H1" inside the tags put **"H2"**. Upon hitting the "refresh" button you will see that the heading is still in larger text but this is slightly smaller than using "H1". Headings in basic HTML can actually come in six different sizes using H1 right through to H6; H1 is the largest and H6 is the smallest.

Structure

It is normal for Web pages to be structured in a similar manner. Although it isn't compulsory this is how the majority of documents are formatted:

<HTML> *(this shows the document is created in HTML)*

<HEAD><TITLE> *(insert your title here)* **</TITLE></HEAD>**

<BODY> *(put your main text here)* **</BODY>**

</HTML> *(this is the end of the document)*

You will see from this that Web pages have two parts, a header section and a body. The header contains the title and other information which is then displayed at the top of your Browser window. Other parts, which won't be covered in this publication are used at the top or the header section to describe your page to search engines. The body of the page is that which appears in the main window of the Browser.

Spaces and Returns

Standard HTML ignores all spaces, tabs and carriage returns in your text. No matter how many of these you insert in your document they will all be combined to produce just a single space in the Browser. You can get around this for some Browsers by enclosing your text with the tags **<PRE></PRE>** which means that it is pre-formatted text. However there are more conventional ways of doing things.

The single tag **<P>** is used to end a paragraph and create a single line break in the Browser Window. The tag **
** will start your text on a new line. However two of these tags will create a line break and three will create two line breaks, etc.

Don't worry about text wrapping because Browsers perform this automatically and page width can be totally ignored.

Rules

A Horizontal line can be created using the **<HR>** tag and entering a few more details. In full:

<HR WIDTH=A% ALIGN=B SIZE=C>

where "A" represents the percentage of the page width that you would like the like to draw, "B" is its position using "Centre", "Left" or "Right" and "C" is its thickness. The default values using the simple <HR> tag is for 100%, centre and 1 (pixel).

Backgrounds

You can apply a colour to all of your body text by using the **<BODY>** tag. For example:

<BODY BGCOLOR="#008000">

changes the background colour to green. This code tells the Browser which RGB combination it should use and you will find a list of the codes for different colours at the site:

www.stars.com/Authoring/Graphics/Colour/

which contains enough colours to get you under way.

Images

Using images on World Wide Web pages requires a bit of an artistic insight. Nevertheless you might want to throw in one or two just for effect. The thing to remember is that the more images you have the longer it will take for your page to load. If it takes too long a casual Browser will probably hit their stop button and disappear from your site, and that is the last you will ever see of them.

The smaller your images are, therefore, in terms of bytes and the fewer you use the quicker your page will load into a normal Browser. So when you are creating your image to place on your page with your image editor make it as small as possible by decreasing the resolution. Also play around with format for your image to find out which creates the smallest image file for an acceptable resolution, is it ***.gif** or ***.jpg**?

The easiest way of displaying an image on your page is to place it with an **<IMG>** tag or more specifically:

<IMG SRC="(image location)">

To show your image at its full size with adjacent text and bottom alignment.

Extra specifications between the IMG and SRC will give you more control over the image:

<IMG HEIGHT=200 WIDTH=300 ALIGN=TOP SRC="myimage.gif">

would display your image as 200 pixels high by 300 pixels wide and align it with the top of the highest item on the line.

It is good practice to include an alternative to the image in text. This is for people who are browsing with the images switched off and will not know what its subject matter is. Again between the **IMG** and **SRC** insert:

ALT="(insert title of image here)**"**

and you won't get many complaints.

Links

This is probably the most important part of your page since the whole idea of the World Wide Web is to give documents another dimension by linking them to other pages. You do this by embedding links to redirect the Browser to another address.

This link could be by way of text, icon or an image. The text, icon or image will normally give some form of indication to the Browser as to where the link will direct them but the URL itself is not normally displayed. Remember, however, that most Browsers will display the address when the mouse is placed over the top of the hyperlink.

To create a link to another page on the World Wide Web insert the following onto your page:

<A HREF="http://www.net-works.co.uk">Net.Works</A>

This will create a hyperlink from the name "Net.Works" on your page and direct the Browser to the home page for "Net.Works". Why not try it out now with your Browser?

You may of course wish to create a link to another of your own pages. This means that you do not have to direct the Browser to another domain, merely another page. You would enter something like:

<A HREF="books.htm">The Book Page </A>

This would direct the Browser to the page *books.htm* within your domain.

You can even embed a link within an image like so:

<A HREF="books.htm"><IMG SRC="book.gif"></A>

In this case the picture of a book called *book.gif* is a link to the page *books.htm*. Somebody clicking on the picture of the book within their Browser will be directed to your books page.

There are many other links that you can put in your page such as to newsgroups, telnet sessions and FTP servers. But perhaps the only other one that you need to know at this point is how to get **mail** sent to you. Do this with strings similar to:

<A HREF="mailto:sales@net-works.co.uk">Sales Department</A>

With most Browsers clicking on the text "Sales Department" will open a "send mail" dialogue box already addressed to sales at net-works.co.uk

Inspiration from Others

Once you are happy that you understand the basics of HTML you can start to play around with your page and make it look a lot smarter. One of the simplest and quickest ways of enhancing the look of your page is to go for a surf yourself. Take a look around the Web and find some pages that you like then save these to your hard disk.

Once off-line, open these pages again using your Browser. Then go to the command line and choose **view source** from the menu bar. Just as when you created your first page a Notepad will open and show you the HTML code behind the page you are looking at in the Browser. From this you will be able to see how the Webmaster has created the page and what HTML codes he has used to get the effects.

You must be careful to stay within the bounds of copyright but it is not beyond the realms of possibility to cut and paste sections of the raw code from their page into your own. If you are only using small sections of the page there should be no problem but do not over do it. If you go too far you may find that the interaction between cyber-police and the uniformed variety is greater than you first thought.

Housing your Page

Now that you have created your first World Wide Web page you will need to find somewhere to put it. For most people the only option will be to put it on somebody else's system. This is because setting up your own server and connecting it directly to the Internet and all it entails would be prohibitively expensive.

For starters you will need quite a powerful computer, a top-of-the-range modem, a permanently open phone line, modifications to your computer to make it a "gateway", probably a router (coming in at a cost of around £750) and a suite of server software. You will also need domain name software so that your computer can navigate the rest of the Web. All of this, and a little bit of consultancy to help you put it all together, could set you back by the better part of £5,000.

So, back to the cheapest way of getting your new page onto the World Wide Web. This is by leasing some space on your access provider's system on their hard disk. In return for hard cash they will set aside a certain amount of disk space for your sole use where you can place all of your files and where other Web users will come to have a look at your page.

Prices very considerably between access providers as to how much they will charge for a certain amount of disk space. Many are giving away **free space** with their Web access packages. But this isn't often much and is always laden with a lot of **conditions**. The main limitation for a normal user would be the fact that virtually no ISP's will allow you to use free space for commercial activities.

So if you want to sell anything or make your fortune on the World Wide Web you are going to have to look elsewhere. Expect to pay around about £5 per Meg for rented space. That should be sufficient for around 7-10 pages on the World Wide Web depending on how many graphics you use.

However there is ever increasing competition between Internet Access Providers and Web Space Providers which are constantly pushing down prices and so you should be able to find cheaper rates by shopping around.

The main advantage of putting your site on a provider system is the speed of connection. Anybody coming to the site will be connected at the same speed as if they were coming to your access provider site.

That is bound to impress other surfers since the speed of access is the major concern to users of the World Wide Web. What is more the company that houses your Web space will probably give you assistance in setting up file transfer protocol software which you will need for uploading your files onto their computer.

Further Reading?

Net.Works publish **Create Your Own Web Site** by Mark Neely. More details can be found on page 112, but I can personally recommend it as a an excellent introduction to the whole subject of Web Site creation.

Chapter 12

Hot Sites

THE BEST THING to do on the Web is to just get out there and have a look around. That's half the fun of it. Nevertheless here is a selection of sites that you might take a look at.

Entertainment

www.disney.com

Loads of video clips from films, books that you can download, interviews and, of course, information on Disney's products.

buildacard.com

Build your own greetings card on-line with the help of the art studio.

www.sony.com/

Sony don't just make radios and television sets. They also own the rights to hundred's of films, music tracks, videos, public broadcasts, and of course games (for their Playstation).

www.lottery.co.uk

If you want confirmation that you haven't yet won the lottery jackpot go to this site and read the latest lottery news.

www.bubble.com/webstars/

Daily forecasts for all star signs to read on-line.

www.leisurehunt.com

On-line booking facilities for over 55,000 places of entertainment in the United Kingdom.

Books

www.thebookplace.com

This site has been set up by Book Data, a company that has been providing bibliographic data to the book trade for more than 10 years.

www.amazon.com

Unlike other bookshops on the World Wide Web, Amazon did not exist before the Web took off. It does not have a single high street store.

www.bookshop.co.uk

Britain's rival to Amazon.

www.bookends.co.uk

An on-line magazine which has weekly top 10's from publishers and reviews the latest titles to be released.

www.gamble.co.uk

A site that has already been mentioned in this publication but is an excellent example of a niche marketing Web site. It not only carries a full selection of books on the subject of gambling but also includes gaming such as chess, bridge, and backgammon. Lots of the books have individual reviews and include a picture of the cover.

Business

www.admarket.com

This is a resource for anybody wanting to advertise or market on the World Wide Web.

www.dmworld.com

Another large resource this time for direct marketeers.

www.fedex.com/

Could this be the way of the future to monitor how parcels are getting on?

www.hm-treasury.gov.uk

Forecasts, reviews and press releases from the Treasury. Also includes Chancellors' speeches.

Motoring

www.carlounge.com

This was the first motoring Web site to hit the Net.

www.carsource.co.uk

This site will notify you when "your car" is available.

www.carshop.co.uk

This is a Web version of Auto Trader.

www.rallyzone.co.uk

Photographs, features and reports from the world of rallying.

Childrens

www.ex.ac.uk/bugclub/

This is the official fan club for everybody who likes things that wriggle and crawl.

www.ravenna.com/coloring/

It bit like painting with numbers on the World Wide Web.

www.yahooligans.com

A Web directory and search engine especially for children.

www.lego.com/

Just as you would expect, lots of pictures of fancy models, a magazine and plenty of competitions for the youngsters.

www.petcat.co.uk

Find out how to care for, feed, groom and play with your cat and if you can't find what you are looking for you can post your questions to the pet cat expert.

Museums and Galleries

www.nhm.ac.uk/

One of the Web's pioneering sites is the Natural History Museum in London.

Mistral.enst.fr/~pioch/louvre/

Lots of images of famous art pieces from gothic to mediaeval and from cubist to pop.

www.icom.org/vlmp/world.html

A directory of Web museums usefully sorted by country.

Glossary

www.moma.org

If you have ever wondered what modern art is all about (and who hasn't?) take a look at this site and see if you can figure it out.

Sport

www.golf.com/

Has maps of international golf courses, tips on playing, the schedules for the professional golf circuits, merchandise, publications to do with golf, etc, etc.

www.cricket.org

It is not exactly Wisden but there are lots of stats and info on the game.

www.nba.com

This is the official site for the NBA with lots of professional basketball news, player profiles, match analysis and results.

eucenter.com/ski/

A good place to start for snow reports and details of events and resorts in Europe.

www.surflink.com

Wave forecasts, surf board shops, and all the rest of the stuff, up-to-date Gnarlies live for.

www.fa-premier.com

Simply the last word in football sites.

www.rugbyclub.co.uk

For oval ball followers.

bit A concatenation of "binary digit". The smallest unit of measurement for computer data.

bps Bits per second. The speed at which data can be transferred between pieces of hardware. You are most likely to come across it in relation to how fast modems work.

Browser

To download and read documents taken from the World Wide Web you need a software program called a browser. The most common are from Netscape, Mosaic and Microsoft.

byte A byte is made up of (usually) eight bits. A byte is the smallest addressable unit of data storage.

client Software on a computer which is used to request information from the Internet. When you call up a web page you are acting as the client, and the computer you have contacted is the 'server'.

DNS Domain Name System. The system which regulates the naming of computers on the Net. The name and network address of every computer connected to the Internet is stored in several large databases which other computers consult so they can translate computer names (like net-works.co.uk and compuserve.com) to numeric (IP) addresses (such as 255.124.64.207).

domain name An Internet identification name which specifies where your computer can be contacted. It is written as a series of letters separated by full stops and slashes; for instance ours is net-works.co.uk. An address will usually consist of a Top Level Domain name, a second-level name and a country code.

download The process of copying a file from one machine (usually the host) to another (usually yours).

FAQ Frequently Asked Questions. This is a document found in most Usenet groups. It will have questions (and answers) that are most commonly asked by newcomers to the group. Read it before you post any questions in a group.

Home Page. The first page of a company's web site and the one you will be taken to as a default. It is also often used as a generic term for the whole web site of a company or individual.

host Another computer on the Internet which allows users to connect to it. An ISP's computer is a host computer.

HTML Hypertext mark-up language. You need to know this language to create documents to go on the World Wide Web.

http Hypertext Transfer Protocol. The way to transfer HTML documents between the client and the Web server (so others can then see them on the WWW).

hypertext Text on your computer screen which you click to take you to another document in the same web site or at another. Hypertext links form the basis of the World Wide Web. When creating a web site the author uses HTML to put up hypertext.

Internet Service Provider (ISP) A company which provides Internet access.

Internet Protocol (IP) One of the many protocols or standards which regulate the way in which information is passed between computers on the Internet.

ISDN Integrated Services Digital Network. It is a network which allows you to send information in a digital form over the existing telephone lines at speeds of 128Kb.

modem MOdulator DEModulator. A device which can send and receive information.

packet The term given to a unit of data sent over a network.

password A secret word or code used, together with your userid, to connect to your account, or to another computer on the Internet.

PPP See SLIP/PPP.

protocol A standard which dictates how computers on a network interact with each other. The most important protocol for Internet computers is TCP/IP.

server (1) Software which is used to provide access to an Internet resource e.g. a Gopher Server. To access the server software, you usually need a client program. (2) The computer which is running the server software.

SLIP/PPP Serial Line Internet Protocol/Point-to-Point. Two different types of software used to connect computers via modem. When you run either SLIP or PPP software on your computer to connect to your ISP's computer, you are assigned an IP address, and become a part of the Internet for the duration of that connection.

TCP Transmission Control Protocol. A protocol or standard which regulates how information is shared between computers on a network.

upload The act of sending files or information from your computer to another computer, usually referred to as a remote host. When you've cre-

ated your own web page, you'll need to upload it onto your ISPs computer before it becomes available to the rest of the Net.

World Wide Web (WWW) World Wide Web. Commonly known simply as 'The Web', it has opened up the Internet to mass world-wide use. All documents on the web are hypertext-based which means they can all be linked together. You pass from one to the next by clicking on a particular word. Could soon become the definition of The Internet.

On-line dictionary of terms

With the WWW having its history steeped in altruism and being closely connected with computer technology, there are hundreds of excellent sites available which give information about computers, the Internet and the Web. One of the best is the *Free Online Dictionary of Computing:*

http://wfn-shop.princeton.edu/ cgi-bin/foldoc

FREE page on the world wide web and 10 hours internet access!

That's your reward for buying

Complete Beginner's Guide to the World Wide Web

Now you've finished reading, you are ready to surf. But as a beginner, you'll want to make sure The Web is useful and fun before you commit yourself to any expense. And, of course, you'll also want to convince yourself that the Superhighway is an easy thing to use and a friendly place to be.

So here is how we can help you further. As a reward for buying this guide, we've arranged for you to receive an Internet package, courtesy of CompuServe, worth over £15. Here's what it includes:

❏ **FREE Internet software including an award winning web browser,**

❏ **10 hours FREE access to The Internet, including the WWW**

❏ **FREE page on the World Wide Web,**

❏ **FREE Membership of CompuServe for one month,**

❏ **FREE CompuServe Information Manager software**

❏ **FREE subscription to the CompuServe Magazine,**

❏ **And, perhaps, more valuable to *The Complete Beginner* is a**

    customer support service (also available on-line)

Why not give it a try, you've nothing to lose!

To: Free.Surfing, Net.Works, PO Box 200,
Harrogate, N.Yorks, HG1 2YR, England

YES, I want to surf The Web! Please rush me the Free Membership Pack which entitles me to 10 hours free access to The Internet, free software and a web page...

Name: _____

Address: _____

_____

_____

_____ Postcode: _____

Please allow 14-21 days delivery. We hope to make you further exciting offers in the future. If you do not wish to receive these, please write to us at the above address.

wwwbk

The Complete Beginner's Guide to Making Money on The Internet

In 1996, businesses clocked up more than £230 million in sales over the Internet. Within one year that figure had risen to £500 million and was still growing almost exponentially!

These on-the-net businesses used the Internet to slash costs; decrease the cost of customer support; reduce purchasing costs; cut marketing expenses and to reach hitherto untapped markets. Their secrets are revealed in this book, so that you can make money on the Internet before your competitors beat you to it.

You'll find answers to the following questions:

- Is the Internet right for my business?
- How can I use the Internet to get and keep customers?
- Can I get started quickly and cheaply?
- What are the potential problems?
- How can I avoid costly mistakes?

It does not matter what type of computer or software you have from IBM, Windows '95, Macintosh or OS/2, you can benefit from this book to make money on the Internet. **Price: ONLY £3.95**

"I would highly recommend this book as both a learning tool for someone contemplating the Internet and for use by the more experienced user as a memory jogger. An excellent publication."
David Siggs, Managing Director, Business Opportunity World

Create Your Own Electronic Office

Home-based business... Cottage industry... Small Office/Home Office (SOHO)... whatever term you use, operating from home, means you escape the stresses, pressures and overheads of a busy town centre office. What-is-more, the time saved by not having to commute will allow you to work more efficiently and spend quality time enjoying yourself.

If this sounds like the kind of independence that you have dreamed of, then this book is for you. With its help, you will:

- Decide whether working from home is for you;
- Equip your office with the right technology to make it efficient from day one;
- Plan your new business and working environment

£5.95

Included are chapters on getting yourself motivated for working by yourself for yourself, how to maintain a healthy separation between your work and private life, and how to present yourself and your new business in a professional manner.

Find What You Want on the Internet

The sheer size of the Internet's information resources is its biggest challenge. There is no central repository of all this information, nor it is catalogued or sorted in ordered fashion.

Find What You Want on The Internet is designed to teach Internet users — from novices to veterans — how to locate information quickly and easily.

The book uses jargon-free language, combined with many illustrations, to answer such questions as:

❑ Which search techniques and Search Engines work best for your specific needs?

❑ What is the real difference between true 'search' sites and on-line directories, and how do you decide which one to use?

❑ How do the world's most powerful Search Engines really work?

❑ Are there any 'special tricks' that will help you find what you want, faster?

ISBN: 1-873668-48-1
Price: £5.95

There is also a bonus chapter covering Intelligent Agents — special high-tech personal search programs that can be installed on your computer to search the Internet on your behalf, automatically.

Complete Beginner's Guide to Word for Windows

Using Microsoft Word is a hit and miss process for a lot of people, and the end results are usually far from satisfying. What-is-more, many of the alternative books available are difficult to understand, and do not focus on the task of getting the job done, leaving you free to write creatively.

The Complete Beginner's Guide to Word for Windows is different. It has been designed and researched by the people who know best - the trainers who teach Word for a living. They understand both beginners and advanced students, and know how to meet their needs.

With clear, step-by-step instructions, and plenty of easy to understand examples, this book guides you to success the easy way. It leaves you free to concentrate on your document instead of getting the program to run properly! **£5.95**

The Complete Beginner's Guide to The Internet

What exactly is The Internet? Where did it come from and where is it going? And, more importantly, how can everybody take their place in this new community?

The Complete Beginner's Guide to The Internet answers all of those questions and more. On top of being an indispensable guide to the basics of Cyberspace,

❑ It is the lowest priced introduction on the market by a long way at a surfer-friendly £4.95. Who wants to spend £30+ on an alternative to find out The Internet is not for them?

❑ It comes in an easy-to-read format. Alternatives, with their 300+ pages, are intimidating even to those who are familiar with The Net, let alone complete beginners!

Price: £4.95

The Complete Beginner's Guide to The Internet tells you:

● What types of resources are available for private, educational and business use,
● What software and hardware you need to access them,
● How to communicate with others, and
● The rules of the Superhighway, or 'netiquette'.

Order form for all books on back page

The Expert's Business Guide to The Internet

The Internet is changing and evolving literally every day, each change bringing with it new opportunities and ideas for promotion and marketing. And this guide helps you explore all aspects of establishing yourself in this huge marketplace.

Written specifically for businesses wishing to establish a strong Internet presence, it takes you through the issues surrounding the development of electronic commerce (the digital economy) by explaining in **non-technical terms** what business on the Internet is all about.

Price: £24.95
including free
updates via the web.

The author closely examines the social dynamics and popular culture of the Net, which will play a large part in any strategy to commercially harness Cyberspace.

● What constitutes acceptable commercial activity on the Net - and what could cause your company to be 'flamed'.
● How to develop an integrated Internet strategy.
● Privacy and Security when dealing with digital cash.

Order using the form on the back page and claim a £5 discount =£19.95

More books by Net.Works

Create Your Own Web Site

The World Wide Web is being trans-formed into an important business and communications tool. Millions of computer users around the globe now rely on the Web as a prime source of information and entertainment.

Once you begin to explore the wonders of the Internet, it isn't long before the first pangs of desire hit – you want your own Web site.

Whether it is to showcase your business and its products, or a compilation of information about your favourite hobby or sport, creating your own Web site is very exciting indeed. But unless you're familiar with graphics programs and HTML (the "native language" of the Web), as well as how to upload files to the Internet, creating your Web page can also be very frustrating!

£5.95

But it doesn't have to be that way. This book, written by an Internet consultant and graphics design specialist, will help demystify the process of creating and publishing a Web site. In it you will learn:

● What free tools are available that make producing your own Web site child's play (and where to find them);
● How to create your own dazzling graphics, using a variety of free computer graphics programs;
● Who to talk to when it comes to finding a home for your Web site (If you have an Internet account, you probably already have all that you need); and
● How to advertise your Web site and attract other Internet users to it.

Book Order Form

Please complete the form USING BLOCK CAPITALS and return to
TTL, PO Box 200, Harrogate HG1 2YR or fax to **01423-526035**

☐ I enclose a cheque/postal order for £_____ made payable to 'TTL'

☐ Please debit my Access/ Visa/Amex Card No:

Book	Qty	Price

Expiry date: ☐☐☐☐

Signature:

Date:

Postage: Over £8 FREE   *Otherwise please add 50p per item within UK, £1.50 elsewhere*

Total:

Title: _____ Initials: _____

Name: _____

Address: _____

_____

Postcode: _____

Please allow 14-21 days delivery.

We hope to make you further exciting offers in the future. If you do not wish to receive these, please write to us at the above address.

Daytime Telephone: _____

wwwbk